FLIGHT PATH

Flight Path

A Search for Roots beneath the World's Busiest Airport

HANNAH PALMER

HUB CITY PRESS
SPARTANBURG, SC

BOOK DESIGN: Meg Reid
COVER PHOTO: © Johnathon Kelso
COVER LETTERING: M.E. Sullivan
COPY EDITOR: Karin Klein
Printed in Dexter, MI by Thomson-Shore

PHOTOGRAPH CREDITS
Page 4 © Joeff Davis
Page 106 © Hartsfield-Jackson Atlanta International Airport
Office of Communications

Library of Congress Cataloging-in-Publication Data

Palmer, Hannah, 1978-
Flight path : a search for roots beneath the world's busiest airport
/ by Hannah Palmer.
Spartanburg, S.C. : Hub City Press, 2017.
LCCN 2016037303 | ISBN 9781938235283
Atlanta Metropolitan Area (Ga.)—Biography.William B. Hartsfield-Atlanta International Airport—Influence. | Atlanta Metropolitan Area (Ga.)—History. | Atlanta Metropolitan Area (Ga.)—Social life and customs. | Atlanta Metropolitan Area (Ga.)—Economic conditions.Clayton County (Ga.)—History, Local.
Fulton County (Ga.)—History, Local.
LCC F294.A853 P35 2017 DDC 975.8/231043092 [B]—dc23
LC record available at https://lccn.loc.gov/2016037303

Supported in part by the Watson-Brown Foundation

Hub City Press
186 West Main St.
Spartanburg, SC 29306
1.864.577.9349
www.hubcity.org
www.twitter.com/hubcitypress

for Guy and Bruno. You're from here, too.

CONTENTS

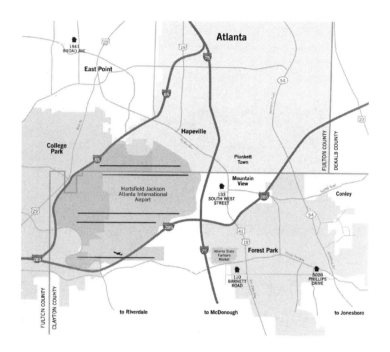

My houses in the Atlanta airport area.

The Kirkwood Neighbors' Organization and my old house.

ONE

TEARDOWN

Despite protests from the Kirkwood Neighbors' Organization and bad press in the local paper, they bulldozed the house where I lost my virginity.

It was a turn-of-the-century farmhouse about a mile from my college campus, with great blue-grey gables framed by two towering cedars at the street. In 1895, the house would have been a suburban retreat, six miles east of downtown Atlanta by streetcar. In 1997, the area had been swallowed by the city but, like most old intown neighborhoods, it retained the green isolation and slow pace of the country. In the back yard, a small bamboo stand hid the beginnings of a creek, while on all sides oaks rippled over sidewalks and asphalt. The summer I lived at 332 Murray Hill Avenue, the nights were noisy with crickets and bullfrogs and the dreamy monotone of the MARTA train.

Technically, it was Mom's house, one of a series of rentals. My mother, a high school-educated waitress, florist, potter, and party girl, moved cheerfully every two or three years during my childhood. Never far, each time just a neighborhood over, to another rental house or crumbly duplex or roach-bombed apartment in a hacked-up Victorian. My mom left my dad, my sister and me when we girls were toddlers and she'd been moving ever since. She moved whenever the lease was up; she moved to break up with boyfriends. In fact, Mom was always moving, never still. Always loading and unloading pots from her kiln, flats of flowers from her truck, or scuba gear from the basement. Mom was forever damp with a fine glow of perspiration, with her rosy cheeks, fabulous cleavage, and moist wisps of hair curling around her face.

She filled each place she rented with stacks of magazines, bottles of perfume, and saucers of seashells and dried butterflies. Wherever she moved, she covered every wall and surface with artwork. My mother was part of Atlanta's vibrant, artsy, gay, post-hippie crowd that created an intown scene in the eighties while white families evacuated to the suburbs. I think she paid only $700 per month for the house on Murray Hill Avenue because the neighborhood was so "transitional"—that's code for transitioning from black to white residents, or the other way around. From Grant Park to Virginia-Highland, Inman Park to Kirkwood, Mom's old stomping grounds have now gentrified into Atlanta's most prized urban real estate.

It was by far the biggest, grandest place Mom had ever rented. The 14-foot ceilings predated air conditioning, so it was cooler to prop open the front and back doors with box fans, pulling the breeze down the wide central hallway, rather than taking chances with Georgia Power. The rooms were uneven hexagons joined by tiled fireplaces and heavy, double pocket doors. To guests, I pointed out the wealth of fireplaces, all six defunct. Everything about the house, from the stone porch columns and thick front door to the wood trim and oblong doorknobs, seemed broader than stability required. It was built to last another hundred years.

Mom arranged her pottery wheel on the side porch and sub-let the two enormous front bedrooms to friends and exes. I was attending college nearby, so I stopped by regularly to escape the dorms, wash laundry, and hang out with Mom's revolving crowd of guests. The large, secluded property was ideal for her extravagant parties.

At one fateful soiree, she seduced a chef, swiftly married him, and embarked on a three month European honeymoon. Her suitors were shocked.

"She's forty-two," I said, shrugging. "Time to settle down."

And so I came to live at 332 Murray Hill Avenue for the summer, basically house sitting and dog sitting rent-free while Mom was on her honeymoon. It was the first time I'd lived with my mother since my parents' divorce, and she wasn't actually there.

Mindy, my best friend from high school, moved in to keep me company and to avoid going home for the summer. We only lived there for a few months, but it seemed longer. It was the summer after our freshman year, and the days were long and eventful. We had no parents, dorm rules, or classes. We had no greater ambition than to live as cheaply and work as many double shifts as possible. Mindy, perpetually tan, barefoot, and grinning, added twinkly lights to the wrap-around porch. I pumped enough gasoline into my red Honda to report to my hostessing job at Mick's: An American Grill. Afterwards, I rambled down the long gravel driveway of Murray Hill at midnight, my all-black uniform plastered with sweat and kitchen grease. I hoped to find Mindy's blue hatchback already parked and cooling. Where were we going tonight? I wondered. Or who was coming over? A breeze seemed to follow me everywhere.

Our landlord, Carol, was the lone authority figure on the premises. Bone-thin and fair-skinned, with that long, stringy hair that doesn't flatter women over thirty, she showed up occasionally to plant pansies and make minor renovations. We received no phone call, no warning that she was coming over. We dashed out to the mailbox in our pajamas and there was Carol, elbow deep in a planter. We watched her through the window, murmuring, "What is she doing here?" We believed she was keeping an eye on us. Or worse—preparing to sell our house.

That summer, between spontaneous rounds of smoothie making, finger-painting, and lying out on the back deck, Mindy and

I continued the work of throwing house parties. Mom would have been proud. Boys spilled out into the back yard, random neighbors showed up and offered us "crack rock." As the hostess, I fell in love with a number of guests, but it was only Jason, a lanky, foul-mouthed video artist I barely remembered from high school, who actually fell in love with me. In August he attended my nineteenth birthday party and celebrated by streaking the crowd and ceremoniously taking a bubble bath with a few friends in the middle of the party.

He cornered me by the refrigerator and invented the world's greatest pickup line: "I miss you because I don't know you yet."

I was startled and amused; he soon had my undivided attention. Jason always called first. He always called back. He pursued me into September, October, November, even after he went back to school in Savannah.

As the year drew to a cold and soggy end, Mom and her new husband were busy scouting for a new home—to buy, not rent. In fact, they planned to leave Atlanta altogether and "start over" in a small, artsy village in the mountains. "Enough of this traffic," she said. "I won't miss the city at all." The newlyweds were gone for weeks at a time while Mindy was spending more and more nights at her boyfriend's place. So Jason stayed with me during Thanksgiving break.

Even though the actual virginity-losing was not the most romantic procedure, the spot where the historic deed took place deserves a memorial plaque. Fortunately, my future husband was already an expert at making me laugh. He had silently resolved to follow me, marry me, put his name on a mortgage next to mine, and he expected me to change my name, birth his babies, and stay with him for life. Assuming all of this in advance, he took great care not to wreck the body squirming underneath him.

Suddenly it was Christmas, and we had to face our parents and sisters and brothers again. The lease was up. Mom and the chef were moving to Tennessee; Mindy and I had to vacate. There was a light, funereal winter rain as we moved out. I remember slipping on the front porch steps as I carried boxloads of books to my car. Within a few months, Mindy was engaged to her boyfriend, a Biblical Studies major, which means I never saw her again. We were the last renters, the last residents of 332 Murray Hill Avenue.

During my remaining time in college, I moved several more times from dorms to apartments to rooms in people's houses where I always felt like a guest. Jason and I squeezed into twin-sized beds in other cities, states, and countries. If I found myself riding MARTA eastbound, I studied the houses passing below the elevated tracks and tried to catch a glimpse of Murray Hill Avenue. Carol had the house painted mustard gold before she put it on the market. I learned to look for the tall back deck and the thicket of bamboo.

In 2001, a developer called The Enclave of Kirkwood, LLC, bought 332 Murray Hill Avenue along with seven other parcels on the street. They proposed to tear down the structures, clear-cut the property, and subdivide it into ten residential lots with ten new single-family homes. But the plans stalled for years for a number of reasons, including a legal issue over a road easement, concerns about the impact on the creek, and a growing protest over plans to demolish the hundred-year-old "historic gem."

I read about these protests while I was living in New York City and working as an entry-level assistant to a literary agent. I was surprised to learn that 332 Murray Hill Avenue was a "landmark structure," a "rare example of Queen Anne style architecture," and the childhood home of an actress named Jane Withers, a child star contemporary of Shirley Temple who later starred with Elizabeth Taylor, Rock Hudson, and James Dean in the movie *Giant*. I had never given a thought to the many lives that must have passed through the place since 1895. To me it was the house where I dyed my hair black in the bathtub and filled the fridge with Jello shooters. The house where Mom, Mindy, and I all found the men we would marry.

The newspaper said that squatters had vandalized the interior of the house during the extended legal negotiations among the Kirkwood

Neighbors' Organization, City of Atlanta Department of Watershed Management, and the developers. I wondered what vandalized meant. Broken windows and graffiti? Gutted for scrap metal? I imagined the worst. Not that it mattered to The Enclave of Kirkwood, LLC. The house was a teardown—the parcel's location held the value.

My dread was short-lived. A week later, I sat at my desk on Fifth Avenue, nine hundred miles from Kirkwood, hunched behind a large computer display, pretending to work while reading online about this saga. The follow-up article announced, "Historic Home Toppled, Despite Neighbors' Protests."

I pitied the protestors. The photo accompanying the article made them look like a handful of NPR-loving birdwatchers who had bravely prevailed over the local crack trade only to be defeated by new-money developers who couldn't tell a Queen Anne from a late Victorian. But I knew the real reason their campaign had failed. It was me. 332 Murray Hill Avenue was doomed because it had been my home. I had sealed its fate when I kissed my future husband on those front steps.

In my mind, the house's demise was part of a pattern. Every house I had ever lived in had been destroyed. The bungalow in Mountain View. The house my Dad moved us to on Barnett Road. The tract home in Forest Park. Sometimes it felt like a giant eraser followed me from place to place, wiping away my past. It rezones the landscape into warehouses, airport runways, and in one case, a CVS Pharmacy. There's a spot in the cosmetics aisle where I estimate my childhood bedroom used to be. I slept there for thirteen years, and now the view from my bedroom window features an array of lip color, thousands of small tubes suspended in midair. I sleepwalk to the parking lot. Whose idea was this? Whose dream have I wandered into?

I BEGAN THINKING ABOUT the Murray Hill house when I was pregnant with our first son. Jason and I, now married and in our early thirties, were living in a 1940s bungalow on the southside of Atlanta, in a neighborhood not far from where we both grew up. Property values all over the city were in a state of collapse. The same houses on our block that had sold for $150,000 when we were buyers were now bank-owned foreclosures, listed at $20,000 and less. Yet we were resolutely pouring money into our tiny two bedroom/one bath house, renovating to make space for the baby.

By this time, the Murray Hill house had been gone for five years, its demolition coinciding with the peak of Atlanta's real estate frenzy in 2006. Back then, I had digested the news with a shrug. The eraser strikes again. But now, with a child on the way, the nesting instinct presented itself as a panicked curiosity about my lost houses. They began haunting me.

I persuaded Jason to drive by The Enclave of Kirkwood, expecting the development to be a fully established cluster of luxury homes with at least two or three on the market. I planned to gather flyers from the More Information boxes out front and laugh at the asking prices.

But this is not what we found at all. As we drove down the familiar street, I was lost. The city was recovering from a weeklong ice storm and crusty snow still clung to the shaded outlines of houses. This Murray Hill Avenue didn't match the summery scenes of my memory.

"You've passed it," I said. "Go back."

Jason kept the truck rolling slowly down the block.

"No, it's up here," he said, gesturing to a large wooded lot. "There's the driveway."

Instead of hosting million dollar nouveau-Craftsmans, the huge lot was vacant. Only vacant isn't the word—there was a jagged, leafy crater where the house had been, rimmed with overgrown debris, gray islands of snow, and No Trespassing signs.

At first I didn't recognize the place, almost refused to recognize it. There was no way they had torn down the house and failed to redevelop the land. That would be a waste too dumb for even the dumbest developer. But the bamboo grove was a dead giveaway. I had to get out of the truck and walk the entire length of the block.

It looked like a hasty demolition—they hadn't even graded the land or marked out the new plots. Jason didn't hesitate to hurdle the orange mesh construction barrier and tromp into the ruins of the foundation. I stopped myself from nagging him and just paced a dry patch of sidewalk, my hands jammed deep in the pockets of my overcoat. As I panned the block, the details of the place gradually came into focus. The long gravel driveway had been rutted by bulldozers. The two tall cedars that had flanked the entrance to the house were still in their places. Somehow, a thin ivy-covered trellis in the front yard had survived the demolition. And then I recognized the yucca plant by the stone steps where we had kissed for the first time. The spiky, tropical plant seemed weirdly out of place, which made the whole scene click in my mind.

Atlanta is full of these half-realized subdivisions, frozen in a state of anticipation, but never built because the financing fell through, the buyers vanished. But this gaping, leaf-strewn pit was a particular insult to me. A warning. They tore it down for no reason. If this could happen to a hundred-year old "gem," it made everything seem disposable.

Why had we come back here? What kind of fools would move to Atlanta to create a home? We planned to grow old in our house, even as we paced the ruined site of our courtship. Maybe I am cursed. Or maybe this is an Atlanta phenomenon.

My city is a young city, recently named and renamed, burned and rebuilt. I should say that by "Atlanta," I mean Metro Atlanta, a sprawling confederation of ten counties and eighty distinct cities, all welded together by interstate highways and populated by people who are not from Atlanta. In business meetings and social gatherings, small talk begins with one of two questions, the first concerning the traffic, and the second asking where you're from. Every time, a Southern drawl slips into my answer: I'm from here. Still, I would be hard-pressed to point out exactly where *here* is.

My feet were getting cold and I worried that we looked like trespassers. We were, in fact, trespassing. How would I explain myself?

Could I say that this was once my home? I had lived here only a few months. Jason joined me on the sidewalk and passed me a brick from the wreckage. I set it in the floorboard of the truck.

I fill these pages, knowing the eraser follows me. I intend to fortify my house.

TWO

BLUEPRINTS OF THE

AIRPORT

Welcome to Bellamy Printing. Your source for printing, copies, business cards, banners, blueprints, three-ply continuous forms, logo design, vinyl vehicle graphics, wedding invitations and sundry screen-printed promotional items. Located just one mile south of McDonough Square. Which is twenty-six miles south of Atlanta (Comfortably South of Atlanta, was the marketing tagline of their Chamber of Commerce). This print shop was a windowless steel box on a tufted patch of red dirt.

Shortly after arriving in McDonough, I walked in the door of Bellamy Printing and politely asked if the owner was available. I left thirty minutes later with a $10-an-hour job in "typesetting." My first job in printing. My first job since I had left the uncomfortable north. Welcome back.

A month before that, Jason and I had driven from Brooklyn to Atlanta without stopping to sleep. My best friend Jenny left us the keys to her father's fishing cabin. We arrived in the dark and missed the turnoff and had to maneuver the trailer holding all our possessions in and out of a neighboring driveway. We were bickering with exhaustion and transfixed by the black pastures and blinding headlights streaking down the two-lane. Ghost deer appeared at the roadside, preparing to dart across. Where was this cabin anyways? The address was not a street, but a highway in McDonough, Georgia.

You hear outsiders—TV news anchormen, Atlanta transplants— pronouncing it just a little bit wrong. Mick-Dunnugh. Ugh. Like some kind of phony brogue. Locals say it MACK-Donna. Like a husband and wife.

Still basically newlyweds, we were crashing here until we could find jobs and a place to rent in Atlanta. We would spend October emailing resumes, housebreaking our new border collie puppy, and fishing for catfish with dog food. By November, the fresh air and golden foliage wasn't cutting it. Jason and I were counting out nickels and dimes to put gas in our '87 Volvo, whose muffler was affixed to the undercarriage with a wire coat hanger and busted hood hinges that had been tack-welded into place at a Jiffy Lube in Ontario the previous summer. We needed jobs.

Hence, Bellamy Printing. I started immediately. The owner, Tommy, a stiff-legged little rooster, was waiting for me at 7:30am. Late thirties, curly mullet, socks jacked up to his shins, polo shirt tucked into his shorts like he was headed for the golf course, which he was. His best feature, I presume, in both business and romance, was his big brown eyes, which his square wireframe glasses magnified to Disneyesque proportions. I would soon learn that he had a goofy/ seductive way of dropping his voice to a low drawl while looking over those glasses and asking you real nice to take care of something while he disappeared to play golf.

Tommy led me through the perfunctory reception area—fax machine, fake plants, books of wedding invitations, paper samples— introduced me to the time clock, the break room, and Dawn, the sole member of the graphics and typesetting department. My career as a graphic designer had begun.

✢ ✢ ✢

MCDONOUGH, GEORGIA, THE GERANIUM City, county seat of
Henry County, is a fine example of what Jenny called "whitey shitbasket." That is, cheap imitation culture served up for a grateful mass audience. Like wall-to-wall beige carpeting or another Walmart on the next
exit, it seems like a good idea in the beginning, but expires quickly.

In 2004, when I moved back "home" to the South, McDonough
was completing its decades long transformation from rural outpost,
once used as a backdrop in *Smokey and the Bandit*, to sprawling
exurb of Atlanta. With its vinyl-clad subdivisions and chain-store
BBQ, McDonough seemed like the opposite of Brooklyn. During
the short time I was there, I did my part in boosting Henry County's
rank, yet again, to the top fifteen of the fastest growing counties in
the nation. McDonough's population jumped from 8,500 in 2000 to
15,500 in 2005.

I am not from McDonough, but the town was full of people I grew
up with. It was odd to be there, in a spanking-new strip mall, ordering
hot wings, and recognize some girl you went to elementary school
with in your hometown. *Oh you moved down here, too?* Of course.
Everyone from Forest Park moved there. McDonough was the town
where all the white people of my hometown relocated, the latest stop
in the southward exodus from Atlanta. And yet we acted surprised to
find each other here, as if we all had made the decision to flee inde-
pendently, spontaneously. Ask almost anyone in McDonough where
they were raised and they will tell you: Forest Park, before it changed.
By this, they are hinting at the decline of our hometown, though
they're not sure how to put it into words.

Jason and I grew up in Forest Park, just like our parents. It used to
be populated by lower-middle-class white Baptists and Methodists,
and small, well-contained pockets of black African-American families
carrying on their parallel communities. Once a middle-class white
suburb, Forest Park had undergone a dramatic racial shift in a short
period of time. In 2003, a Harvard study stated the Clayton County
school system, where I graduated in 1996, as experiencing the "fastest
resegregation nationwide."

Now Forest Park was a fragile hodgepodge of low-income renters, truckers, and itinerants. The Vietnamese, Mexican, and other minority families that remained were left to deal with failing schools, plummeting property values, industrial pollution, tasteless development, and local governments comically ill-equipped to make sense of any of the above. For years, I thought the mass migration from Forest Park to McDonough was white flight, that people wanted to be "comfortably south" of people that didn't look like them. But having arrived in the Promised Land, I started to think there was more to it than racial anxiety. It was the first time I started to think about the economic engine of the city itself: its enormous and devouring airport. The flight path carved an invisible freeway over Forest Park.

When people asked Jason and me why we quit our jobs in Manhattan, relinquished our apartment in Brooklyn, and moved back to the South, we could shuffle a whole deck of good reasons and still tell the truth. Because we missed Waffle House and Chick-fil-A. For the warmer weather. Because we wanted to get a dog, and a dog needs a yard. So we could afford studio space. So we could afford to work less. To slow the painful drip of phone calls from our parents, brothers, and sisters back home, telling us about football games, dance recitals, birthday parties, and baby showers we'd missed. So that we could someday, maybe, consider buying a house. Because we couldn't imagine raising kids without all these things. It certainly wasn't for this, for the traffic and the sprawl, for low-paying jobs and awkward reunions.

What we got was culture shock. Where Brooklyn was old and grimy, cold and compact, Henry County was the direct opposite. We were isolated by the glimmering heat and the sprawl, segregated in cars, in offices, in cul-de-sacs. McDonough felt like the refugee settlement of a conquered tribe. The cheap houses were just tents, the storefronts were like a movie set, all façade. It didn't have to last long.

✤ ✤ ✤

DAWN WAS THE TYPE of woman who would get along well with my stepmother. Crafty Southern ladies, I imagined they both knew the same quilt shops and banana pudding recipes. Dawn had five sons and a tall, wide body that seemed built for boy-mothering and bear hugs. As a matter of introduction, she asked my maiden name.

"You're a Slagle?" she asked, grinning.

"Yeah, that's my Dad's family."

"Get out."

"You know them?"

"They were my next door neighbors on Shellnut Drive! Bobby and Jesse and David and Dan?"

"Yep. Those are my uncles."

Tommy strutted over to the coffee pot.

"Y'all know each other?" he said.

By now, Dawn had me clutched to her chest. "Tommy, you done good hiring this one. She's from good people. I grew up with her family in Forest Park."

"Forest Dark," he smirked.

It was a comment I understood immediately. Admitting you were from Forest Park, or Clayton County in general, was akin to saying you were from the projects.

Dawn rolled her eyes. "Aw, you talk bad about it now, but when I was a kid, it was just like Beaver Cleaver."

"You're gonna show her how to copy plans first, okay?" he said.

Dawn arched an eyebrow.

"Yes sir," she said. And then, to me, "Gawd, you look just like your daddy."

I WASN'T A REAL graphic designer, but I knew enough about desktop publishing and web design to fake it. Because I had stayed in Atlanta for college, which always felt a little too close to my parents and high school friends, I took off for New York City almost immediately after graduation. Jenny already had an apartment in Greenpoint and she not only offered me an air mattress-sized corner, she felt reasonably sure that I could land a job at the magazine where she worked as an art director.

"You get about three months," she warned, "where you have that new-to-New York City glow and everybody loves you."

I planned to use it wisely. I visited her offices in Rockefeller Center during my first week. Met her friend, also from the Atlanta suburbs, who was leaving a tiny shotgun apartment on Graham Avenue for a bigger place in Dumbo. She asked me if I had the $800 deposit and first month's rent. The checks I'd received for graduation just covered it. And like that, armed with nothing more than an English degree and a laptop I could barely operate, I had a job in publishing and a place in Brooklyn. I was twenty-one years old.

Before I could accept the magazine job, I was recruited to a startup publishing company that was producing e-books. It sounds like a peculiar career move now, but during the summer of 2000 the streets of Manhattan were teeming with fresh graduates enlisted to helm a legion of dot-com ventures and new media startups. Magazines were old media. Everyone my age was working for a website, pioneering some new technology or digital service. Pushing around manuscripts as a traditional editorial assistant seemed boring in comparison to designing multimedia content that with any luck, would get us sued and help define the future of electronic media.

At the time, Williamsburg and Greenpoint were still working class neighborhoods and Bedford Avenue was just beginning to resemble an art school campus. Despite the all the Pabst Blue Ribbon and trucker hats, we were yuppies in the eyes of the Polish, Italian, Puerto Rican and Hasidic families that lived there. A band of outsiders, we gathered in the writhing courtyard of PS1 and shouted over the thudding house music, drank El Presidente at Enid's in the slow summer dusk, found rooftop views of the East River to watch the Fourth of July fireworks, all the while gossiping about venture capital, going public, getting funding from Apple or Annenberg or the MacArthur Foundation. The summer soundtrack was the incessant calliope of the Mister Softee truck.

I could barely keep up. I earned blisters on my heels from all the walking. I was surprised by the heat and reek of summer in the city, but also by the carved mangos on a stick sold by a Peruvian at the subway entrance. Brooklyn was as humid and hot as summer in the South, only without an air-conditioned car to seal off the world. Pressed up against sweaty commuters on the train to Union Square, I still had that happy, new-to-New York feeling that at least we're all in this together.

At the same time, I stewed over differences in Yankee etiquette. I never got used to the way New Yorkers greeted you with a handshake and this persistent, "What do you do?" (I just graduated. I didn't actually do anything yet.) Even more offensive was the way Ivy League types introduced themselves by alma mater, as in, "Brice, Harvard '99" and "Ethan, Princeton 2000."

Everyone had an elevator pitch, a personal brand, and they were selling it hard. I learned to strike a balance when I said I was from Atlanta. Too much drawl and they assumed I was an idiot. Not enough Southern charm and I would be instantly forgotten, lumped in with the rest of vanilla Middle America beyond the Hudson River.

In New York City, a city of migrants, there was cultural currency in being from somewhere else, somewhere real. I wanted to distinguish myself, but really I was from the suburbs, not a cotton plantation. What did it mean to be Southern and a Southerner?

First, it was the food. It surprised me that in a city where you can locate obscure international goods on every corner, I could not find something as simple as sweet tea. It made me homesick, this scarcity of biscuits and cornbread. And collards, which I never liked all that much until I started cooking them myself in Greenpoint.

I didn't learn to cook until Jason moved in with me. He found a job in a Times Square production house where he was dubbed "Hayseed" for his thick Southern accent. He rode his BMX over the

Williamsburg Bridge, made friends everywhere he went. He hunted down a vendor in Chinatown that sold green, raw peanuts and he started boiling them for hours in our kitchen. He was home embodied, everything I missed about Atlanta in one person.

I felt this most strongly on September 11th as we held hands and watched the twin towers burn from McCarren Park. We drifted over to a crowd of neighbors, all of us chatty and animated with inane speculation and the uneasy pride that we were witnessing something historic, but hey, just another day in New York City. Then the first tower twisted and buckled and the talking stopped. People screamed and staggered. I saw a bronze pit bull on a leash continue sniffing the ground as if nothing had changed. I turned to Jason and we ran. No one stuck around to watch the second tower fall.

With that collapse, the venture capital and dot-com jobs vaporized. Jason and I took turns riding out unemployment, freelancing and finding new, more traditional jobs. We were married in Atlanta, but drove a carload of wedding presents "home" to Brooklyn. A pressure cooker for greens, a crockpot for peanuts. We spent our first years as a married couple in that three-room apartment in Brooklyn. Saturday mornings, Jason pedaled me on his handlebars down Manhattan Avenue to the Peter Pan doughnut shop.

My boss told me that everyone in New York City was looking for a job, a place, or a lover. That once you had all three, you were done with the city. All along, Jason and I agreed that New York was temporary, like grad school. That after a few years working in video production and publishing, we would "graduate" and take our fancy resumes back home to the South. The idea was to experience the world's greatest city in our twenties and get out before we got jaded. I wanted to escape before we loved it too much to leave.

THE FISHING CABIN WASN'T a cabin at all. It was a brick ranch house built in the late 1970s. Its long, rectangular floor plan contained a two-car carport, wood-paneled kitchen with breakfast nook, a wide orange-carpeted living room, three bedrooms, and two baths. From the back deck, you could pretend you were in the woods. The pines helped muffle the sustained high note of highway traffic.

The house was situated on a stretch of Highway 81 that had once been in the boondocks, but was quickly surrounded by residential development. This is a variation of a sentiment we heard repeated so often it could've been McDonough's tagline: "When we moved out here, it was country!" Tommy's version was, "We've been here since it was nothing but kudzu." There might be a horse or two in a fenced off lot, but the animals seemed decorative. Part of the sales pitch.

It would be better if this were a fishing cabin in the woods. Highway 81 had become a slow-moving parade of juiced-up 4-wheelers.

There was a small lake out back, stocked with catfish. That part was accurate. And we did spend hours swatting mosquitoes out there, with nightfall coming on earlier and earlier. Jason caught fish and threw them back. I practiced Frisbee with the puppy, now named Dairy Queen. We took photos to prove to our friends in New York, and to ourselves, that we were back in the South, doing Southern things.

BELLAMY PRINTING DISTINGUISHED ITSELF in the south Atlanta print-shop market by offering large-scale blueprint copies. This was one of the niche service areas into which Walmart had not yet ventured, so it became a big part of my workday. I fed three-foot wide sheets of paper through a large, standing copier. This machine lived in the "break room," so Tommy and Dawn, Sheryl (the office manager), and Randy (the nineteen-year-old pressman) visited me and the refrigerator throughout the day.

In McDonough, circa 2004, the most common kind of blueprints were residential construction plans (the models have names like Braddock Pointe or Bridlewood), residential landscaping plans, subdivision plans (Waterford Pointe, Stoney Creek, Wellesley Lakes— names with no reference to local history, geography, or lore), church plans, and airport expansion and acquisition plans.

I took my time copying the airport blueprints. For the first time, I could examine the massive, detailed layout of the runways and the surrounding neighborhoods. Here were the names of towns that formed the landscape of my childhood: Forest Park, Mountain View, and Hapeville. There were color-coded areas for acquisition, demolition, and condemnation. I made an extra copy for myself to hang on the fridge at home.

Seeing it all mapped out this way was stunning. Maybe like seeing your house for the first time from above. Your little rooftop and clothesline and nandina bushes and their smudgy little shadows. Your oil stains on the driveway, as judged from some distant orbiting eye. Blurry, but there it is.

The lady who regularly walked into Bellamy Printing to request these copies reminded me of my kindergarten teacher. She was petite and well pressed, with the short, blonde, gel-blasted hair fringe that passed for snazzy professional in this particular time and place. She had a sugary voice and an easy mom-smile that said, *I'm in customer service.* She worked for a law firm.

"So you work for the airport?" I asked as I rolled up a stack of blueprints.

"We're working on a project at the airport," she said. "The Fifth Runway."

She said this with a crinkled up wink, like I should know what she was talking about.

"So what are the plans for?"

"Well, mostly parcels in Riverdale that are still in negotiation."

"What kind of parcels?"

"Businesses. Warehouses. The airport has to acquire all the properties and help them move so they can get that runway built."

"What about the houses?"

I don't think she missed a beat. I was writing up her receipt, just making small talk.

"Houses too. Every seller gets compensated and we help with relocation."

I wanted to tell her about our old house in Forest Park. And my
parents' house in the '70s, when the whole town of Mountain View
was bought by the City of Atlanta. And before that, it was chunks
of College Park and Hapeville, small towns neighboring the airport,
now under the tarmac. All this trivia was bubbling up in me, threaten-
ing to turn into something more than trivial.

"What if someone doesn't want to sell?" I said.

She had answered all these questions before.

"Most everyone sells. I mean, they're right next to the airport, so
eventually all that will be condemned."

"Oh, right. Wow." I swallowed hard. She sounded so sensible. I
handed her the change and the rubber-banded rolls of copies.

DID I MENTION THAT JENNY'S DAD died in this "cabin"? She hadn't
spoken to him in years, so the house—her inheritance—sat shuttered
and stale. In exchange for free rent, we offered to clear out the remaining furniture, scrub the pine paneling of mold, and tear down the ivy
that was overtaking the side of the house. Basically get it ready to be
a rental property. Sponging bleach on those walls was the first time I
realized that a house urgently needed to be lived in. Without the constant flow of air and light, maintenance and money, it quickly became
a dead thing, a burden. This work filled Jason's days as I made copies at Bellamy Printing. It was my first glimpse of the tireless, proud,
sweat-streaked homeowner he would become.

"It's there, if you want it," Jenny had said. "But I'm warning you,
the place is totally shitbasket. I can't believe you're leaving Brooklyn
for this."

I stuck with the theory that Jason and I were happy in Brooklyn, at
home as long as we were together, and we'd be happy in McDonough.
But it was hard.

Jenny's dad had lived here alone, so when a heart attack killed him,
it was a few days before the neighbors began to wonder about his

parked car and came over and found him in his easy chair. I imagine the TV was still blasting, but one starts to embellish.

All this we learned from the neighbors' adult daughter. She was tall and gaunt with heavy makeup and had one of those walkie-talkies that chirped incessantly from her bony hip.

"My daddy cleaned it all up and took care of that chair," she told us. "He didn't want the girls to have to fool with it."

At first, I thought she was sent over on reconnaissance, to see what kind of renters were unloading into "Richard's place." The longer she talked, the more I began to think she was lonely and just liked to tell stories. Lots of stories, delivered rapidly, with little discernible connection between them. When she finally left, Jason and I sat on the floor tussling with the dog. Jason explained what he had recognized right away, that this woman had the distinct chatter and bobble-headed figure of a meth head. It made sense that she returned home to McDonough while her parents looked after her little girl.

I TRY TO REMEMBER THINGS about McDonough in 2004 and I think of cars, hot traffic on I-75, and acres of parking lots. In my memory, Bellamy Printing casts a slim hedge of shade on the sun-parched blacktop. Randy and Sheryl stand there smoking, the large bay doors of the pressroom open behind them.

Here's what was in the parking lot: Sheryl's Ford Explorer, navy blue. She had a mini dreamcatcher hanging from the rearview mirror. Dawn's Chevy Trailblazer, golden brown. Randy's shiny black Honda Civic with chrome accents. It had a huge chrome exhaust pipe. Randy lived with his grandparents, allowing him to drop his entire paycheck into custom accessories for this car. Tommy's towering blue truck/SUV mutant Chevy Avalanche. I quietly renamed it the Hedgehog. And a crusty, blue, 1987 Volvo. My hand-me-down, acquired in Brooklyn, piece of junk. These cars were like outfits, our aspirations and priorities on display. At Bellamy Printing I designed a number of "In Loving Memory" decals that we cut on the vinyl plotter and carefully applied to truck windows.

On all sides of the building are cleared lots where turquoise pipes jab out of the Martian dirtscape, ready to become toilets. That's the other thing about McDonough that dominates every memory—the frenzy of construction and all those blueprints. I think of surveying crews, grading crews, and asphalt trucks. The signs announcing what was "Coming Soon"—luxury homes from the $180s, retail opportunities, a new CVS Pharmacy.

The biggest construction project of all was happening at the airport. People used the term "The Fifth Runway" like a concept I should already know, like The Fourth Wall or The Third Rail. The premise of the thing was equally abstract: build a bigger runway to Atlanta's already landlocked and congested airport. Where would it go? You would have to move mountains, highways, waterways, and neighborhoods.

And that was the plan. The $1.28 billion project transferred twenty-seven million cubic yards of landfill—in some places, that's eleven stories of dirt—to create the new landing strip. They would need a five-mile conveyor belt that looks like a kiddie coaster winding through Riverdale, delivering seven tons of dirt every hour, every day.

The runway would have to extend over I-285, the notoriously clogged Atlanta "Perimeter," requiring an unprecedented runway/bridge combo capable of supporting a million-pound aircraft landing on top while ten lanes of traffic moved a few dozen feet below.

The first new runway since 1984 would be a major public relations opportunity. The superlatives beg for citation: "World's largest runway bridge," "Most important runway in the world," "One of the largest construction undertakings in Georgia's history." At completion, Atlanta would boast one of the few airports in the world able to accommodate triple simultaneous jetliner landings.

Consider the acquisition of 280 parcels of land to assemble approximately 420 acres needed for this slab of concrete. When you read "parcels" and "properties," think gas stations, restaurants, office buildings, industrial warehouses, churches, apartment complexes, elementary schools, and row after row of houses, each one a tiny pressure cooker.

I have trouble picturing Flat Rock Creek, the source of the Flint River, routed underground. Sullivan Creek in a ten- by twelve-foot box culvert, or a square, concrete drainage pipe. And what should be done with the 340 graves in the Union Bethel AME Church Cemetery? Eventually, the dead would be delicately "disinterred" from the bright orange clay by a team of archaeologists and transferred to a site one mile away in Riverdale. Though the tiny Flat Rock Cemetery and Hart Cemetery remained encircled by the grounds of the airport, this African-American graveyard was all but abandoned and few protested the relocation.

Try to estimate the cost of all the acquisitions and relocations, the contracts with architects and designers, geologists, archaeologists, attorneys and analysts. The reams of blueprints! In its very dismantling of the landscape, this runway project was employing a whole city of experts and generating a vast economy all its own. It cost around $1.2 billion to build this one runway. Consider the gargantuan investment, and then assume that the return on investment must be exponentially bigger.

This is how I began to think of the airport as the eraser.

Atlanta's "Fifth Runway," officially named 10-28, sounded impossible, or at least, maniacally ambitious. But there was a plan for all of this. I had missed the details, I guess, because I was busy trying to get out of Atlanta, and then busy trying to "make it" up north. Now that I was back, I couldn't miss the trail of airplanes lined up overhead. Even in rural McDonough, "comfortably south" of the runways, they were a fixture in the sky, more constant than the stars.

THREE

WORLD'S BUSIEST

A nd so I started looking critically at the airport for the first time in my life.

When you grow up in Atlanta, you take it for granted that every airport is as colossal as ATL. I thought all airports had hundreds of identical gates spanning the alphabet: A Gates, B Gates, C, D, E, and T Gates, all smartly linked by an internal subway system. I thought all airports were home to Delta, one of the world's largest commercial airlines, and served as primary hub to multiple other major airlines. It seemed only natural that all major airports would be conveniently connected by train to the central business district of their anchor city, like downtown Atlanta, which was only eleven miles away.

I assumed much of this because in every other respect, Atlanta didn't seem like a real city. When I was growing up, Atlanta felt distinctly anti-urban, more a collection of sleepy suburbs and tidy malls than the cities I saw bursting with excitement on television. Before the Olympics, Atlanta couldn't compare to other major American cities in terms of population density or diversity. We didn't have the vibrant downtown, the street life or museums, the waterfront or skyline that defined New York City, Chicago, Miami, or San Francisco. So it was unexpected that a Southern capital should emerge in this one area—commercial aviation—to dominate every other city in the world.

By the time I was in my twenties, I had experienced this first-hand. Flying back and forth to Atlanta, I spent the night on the floor of the cramped gates of LaGuardia and Newark, boarded a rickety rolling stairway on the tarmac in Salt Lake City, and skateboarded the length of Orlando's tiny terminal. I was puzzled by the complex of travelators and shuttle buses I had to navigate to change gates in Philadelphia and Detroit. I was shocked to peer out from my window seat on the descent into Chicago O'Hare and San Francisco and see how close the runways were to open water, or right on top of tightly gridded neighborhoods.

I had seen a handful of airports and found that none of them, except maybe Denver and Charles de Gaulle, could compare to Atlanta in terms of scale and efficiency. But where, I wondered, was DEN and CDG's underground "plane train" between terminals? Why were both so distant from the city? Why were all my flights out of the northeast delayed or oversold, paralyzed by wind and ice?

I learned that there is nothing on earth like Hartsfield-Jackson Atlanta International Airport.

Atlanta is the home of Coca-Cola and twenty other Fortune 500 companies, Nobel Peace Prize winners Dr. Martin Luther King, Jr. and President Jimmy Carter, cultural icons from *Gone With the Wind* to Outkast, but the first thing anyone will tell you is that we have the world's busiest airport. Invest Atlanta, the city's redevelopment authority, produced a one-pager of winning facts about the city. It includes stats about the film industry, colleges and universities, major employers and government agencies like the Centers for Disease Control and Prevention. All of it is made possible because of the headline in bold at the top of the page: Atlanta's Hartsfield-Jackson International Airport is the world's busiest.

Atlanta earned the title in 1998, shortly after hosting the Centennial Olympic Games. It's held that distinction ever since, beating out fierce, ongoing competition from Chicago, Beijing, Dubai, and London. In 2014, Hartsfield-Jackson averaged a quarter million passengers each day, roughly 2,500 daily arrivals and departures. That's something like three flights per minute, every single day.

Our mega-airport has grown into the world's busiest and along the way it became the economic engine for the entire Southeast region. In 2014, Hartsfield-Jackson boasted a direct economic impact of more than about $32.5 billion for the Metro Atlanta economy, which means Atlanta's gross domestic product is larger than that of thirty states. And 63,000 people work at the airport, making it the largest employer in the region.

The airport is the reason why Atlanta ranks third in the nation as a headquarters for Fortune 500 companies. Over the last sixty years, the airport is what distinguished Atlanta from its Sunbelt siblings in the rapidly urbanizing south. Atlanta's airport-fueled economy is the reason why a whole generation migrated here for jobs after WWII— instead of say, Birmingham or Charlotte—after returning from the war. Directly or indirectly, the airport is the reason why Jason and I could find jobs and cheap rent in Atlanta too.

Why Atlanta? Geographically, Atlanta lies at a centerpoint of global aviation. The city is within a two-hour flight of 80 percent of the United States population, and it's well connected to Central America, South America, and Europe. The weather is predictably mild year round. Unlike other travel hubs such as New York City and Chicago, which split passengers between two and three airports, Atlanta consolidates all its traffic at Hartsfield-Jackson.

There have been three major incarnations of the Atlanta airport. In 1925 it was Candler Field, just prop planes inside a racetrack on the edge of the countryside. Named for Asa Candler, the multimillionaire who established the Coca-Cola Company, it grew as a stop on the postal route. In the 1940s, Atlanta Municipal Airport expanded as the busiest in the nation. In 1961, Atlanta's "jet age" terminal opened, the biggest passenger terminal in the country.

At the grand opening of each new terminal, Atlanta touted the most advanced aviation facilities of the time. In each case, these new terminals were overwhelmed and obsolete within a few years. Airport planners raced to adapt to the demands of commercial aviation, scrambling to accommodate more passengers every year. Their forecasts consistently underestimated the demand, both from passengers and new airlines.

The 1961 airport featured a nifty arrangement of gates, like spokes of a wheel, that was criticized for its confusing layout. The two main runways formed a giant "X," a pattern that could not be duplicated or extended for expansion. When confronted with the problems of the overcrowded new airport, then-Mayor William B. Hartsfield quipped, "They'll all just have to scrooch up, like five folks on a park bench built for four!"

Some bold planning and design decisions in the 1960s set Atlanta on the path to becoming the world's busiest airport for decades. A 1964 master plan for the airport proposed scrapping the entire layout for a reconfigured airfield that increased the land area fivefold. Instead of the conventional criss-cross runways, which maximized the use of land but created traffic jams on the tarmac, planners proposed a series of parallel east/west runways. Instead of starfish-shaped terminals with gates clustered on every arm, the new terminal would be linear and modular, a repeatable pattern to allow for organized expansion over time. The airport would be set up as a flexible grid, a traditional urban form that has accommodated growth from Manhattan to Savannah.

In 1980, these plans came to fruition with the opening of the modern "Central Passenger Terminal Complex" at the newly christened William B. Hartsfield Atlanta International Airport. Mayor Maynard Jackson, who would eventually share these naming rights with his predecessor, oversaw the complete overhaul of the airport. The new terminal was designed to correct the chaos with a super-sized grid system of runways running east to west and gates north to south, connected by an underground train. In the last thirty years, Concourse E and the international terminal have been added to the west, along with the fourth and fifth runways to the south. The scalable arrangement, though less aesthetically inspiring, has proven more durable. Today, its highly efficient parallel runway system can accommodate multiple simultaneous takeoffs and landings. Dubai, Istanbul, and Beijing have all studied and attempted to replicate this layout.

At 4,700 acres, the airport is enormous, but nowhere near as big as the largest in the world. In Saudi Arabia, King Kahlid International Airport is 78,000 acres. The Atlanta airport's status as the world's busiest in passenger traffic on its relatively small site is testament to its incredibly efficient layout and operations, central location, and legacy of innovation in aviation.

What does it mean to be the world's busiest airport? Many major world airports are in a race for this title. Airports that are much bigger, newer, and more elegant are all working constantly to build capacity and win more of those passengers and flights. The only way Atlanta stays ahead is by constantly planning and expanding. The airport has been focused on expanding and building nonstop for the last eighty years.

There's an old adage: "Whether you're going to heaven or hell, you have to change planes in Atlanta." Hartsfield-Jackson has grown primarily as a hub, not a destination. As much as 60 percent of the hundred million travelers flowing annually through the airport never leave it; they simply connect to other flights. They never see the neighborhoods or imagine there are people living nearby. Even many native Atlantans don't realize that the airport was built on top of neighborhoods or that its expansion has had a devastating effect on the city's southside.

The facility's sheer scale contributes to its mystery. There is no vantage point from which you can appreciate its spectacular expanse. There is no iconic portal, no grand arrival sequence, nothing that might contribute to a sense of place there. The design of the airport includes nothing peripheral to the goal of efficiency. In fact, it is wholly possible that the airport's success depends on achieving precisely that kind of anonymity or blankness. Its singular objective is to provide a clear airfield for moving planes in and out, defining a presence so forgettable that it dodges even the critical eye. Everyone uses the airport. No one sees it.

While the airport provided jobs, it gradually made the southside uninhabitable. The neighbors complain about the nonstop flight noise rumbling in the background, shaking the windowpanes, undermining property values. The economic benefits of the airport have always, somehow, trickled to other parts of the city. You get to enjoy the benefits of the airport only if you have a ticket to fly away.

The "world's busiest" title is a kind of consolation prize for all that's been lost on the southside. As if the airport's negative impacts were justified as long as we can claim, as we have since 1998, to be the biggest and best. Without that Guinness World Records appeal, it's hard to love the airport. The vast acres of surface parking, the soulless architecture, the epic slog through security checkpoints, and—no disrespect to mayors Hartsfield and Jackson—that unwieldy, hyphenated name like a forced marriage…Atlanta's airport doesn't exactly inspire devotion.

One could think of the airport as a hunk of infrastructure like an interstate highway, designed for efficiency and high volume, not romance. It was a lot like Atlanta's other landmarks: our hotels and convention centers, our malls, hospitals, and stadiums. Places that everyone used, but no one loved. No one mourns the malls when they die.

As spring faded quickly into summer, the air conditioner in my old Volvo sputtered out. Sitting in traffic in McDonough, missing Brooklyn bitterly, I thought about Atlanta's unlovable places. How did it become normal to sit in traffic like this, six lanes deep, as far as the eye can see? We have a long track record of building places completely disconnected from the city itself, its urban fabric, and cut off from surrounding communities.

We have the world's busiest airport. So what? If Atlanta wants to grow into something more than just a constellation of busy, efficient, but eminently unlovable places, shouldn't someone measure the airport's cultural impact, count the cost of all that's been lost?

And so I decided to try to find the preserved cemeteries near the Fifth Runway. One Saturday morning, I drove to the airport's operations center on Sullivan Road, a quiet, two-lane road named for Sullivan Creek, which was probably named for some long-gone settler.

There I found Flat Rock Cemetery at the top of a hill, miraculously preserved within the boundaries of the airport. I read the memorials, which were streaked and illegible, tilted and toppled by a hundred years of exposure. A sign told me what the worn headstones could not: "This cemetery, its oldest grave dating to 1877, contains the remains of many of the earliest settlers of the surrounding Flat Rock community."

I wandered the grounds, stepping carefully between graves. It looked like any rural Georgia cemetery. I saw granite obelisks, crosses, and tree trunks. I saw names that sound familiar—Dodson, Turner, Liveoak. I saw graves of Confederate soldiers, headstones marked simply "Mother," and the small graves of buried children.

Faded flower arrangements meant that I was not the only one who had ever visited the cemetery, but that day it felt utterly deserted. I was comforted that the runways, built high on green mounds, form such pockets of stillness, like the eye of a hurricane. Overhead, the ceaseless breeze and the white drone of cruising aircraft seemed to circulate around a frozen, unchanging core.

133 South West Street in Mountain View, my first house.

FOUR

THE RENTERS

Tommy decided we needed uniforms. Purple polos with either Bellamy Printing or BP embroidered over the heart. Dawn had a thick catalog open on her keyboard when I arrived one morning.

"We're supposed to tell him what size we want," she said, ceremoniously dumping the phonebook-sized catalog in my lap. The page featured a ponytailed model sporting a neat three-button shirt with contrasting trim.

"He's serious?" I groaned. "What difference is it going to make what we wear?"

Dawn had introduced me to an expression that her sons called "the flat eye"—an unamused glare that's slightly more sarcastic than an eye-roll. She aimed one at me and said, "Buddy's employees wear polos."

"Buddy's employees probably have health benefits," I said. "Think we could make a case for that?"

All summer long, we'd been losing jobs to Buddy's Blueprints. Their Forest Park location was close to the airport. Tommy had more than once mentioned getting us into "more professional attire" as a strategy to stem the losses.

During these months, Dawn and I were helping litter McDonough with new business cards, flyers, coupons, and printed ephemera. Most of our clientele were small business owners. A fellow acquired a dump truck, a stump-grinder, a pressure washer, or a home inspection license, and his first stop was Bellamy Printing, where we would help him choose a clip art logo for his marketing materials. We got paid for volume, not quality, but cranking out logos had the inevitable effect of making me a better designer, able to execute doodles and navigate software with ease. For the first time, I had a genuine trade, like my dad the welder—a skill I could take anywhere.

As the year progressed, so did my graphic design proficiency. In the spring, there were fairy tale wedding invitations and termite contracts. In the summer, we made high school football programs, vinyl banners for church revivals, and three-ply citations for the Henry County Police Department. Dawn cut back to working part-time, shuffling into the office only when she was short on cash. She spent the balance of her day "junking"—prowling thrift shops and estate sales for her booth at a nearby antiques shop. Her husband drove a school bus for the county benefits plan.

At one point, I remember looking around the parking lot and realizing that no one at Bellamy Printing was making a living except the owners. Sheryl was single and lived at her sister's house. Randy lived rent-free in his grandparents' basement. I was earning half of what I'd made at my last job in New York, and now they wanted me to wear a purple polo shirt to work.

"I don't think I can do it," I told Dawn. "I haven't worn a uniform since Girl Scouts."

"Oh, but these are royal purple," she joked.

"No, really," I said, half-aloud and surprised at my own conviction. "It's time to get out of here."

AFTER FOUR MONTHS OF squatting in McDonough, we signed the lease on a tiny house much closer to Atlanta, in Forest Park. Everyone agreed this was a terrible idea. Our friends in the city. Our family in the suburbs. My co-workers at Bellamy Printing. Many of them had escaped from Forest Park.

"I'm just afraid you're going to lose your edge," said Jenny.

At work, I shared my excitement about the Recreation Center that was within walking distance of our new house. "You're not actually going to swim in that pool, are you?" Tommy asked.

Jason and I created a term for it: Fear of Forest Park. We'd grown up there, in a place where white flight felt like a mandatory evacuation. Kids talked during recess and after school about their families' plans to get out. It was not if but when you were going to move. As our neighbors and church congregation moved to Henry County or beyond, the guys left behind were the ones getting involved in gangs and drugs. The girls became strippers or got pregnant or both. Somehow, we blamed Forest Park, as if the town was a toilet and anyone left there was swirling down the drain. By the time Jason and I decided to rent a house there, almost no one we knew was still in Forest Park. It was a form of rebellion to go back.

Dawn tried to be enthused for us. She squealed over the vintage features of the house, just as I did. She approved the paint chips for each room.

At 800 square feet, this rental house was a cottage really, no bigger than our apartment in New York. Unlike Brooklyn, it had a deep backyard where our dog could chase Frisbees or nap in the shade of pecan trees. And a detached garage where I parked my first print-shop acquisition—an antique letterpress about the size of a Volkswagen Beetle. I loved the hardwood floors and crystal doorknobs and the giant camellia bush that plopped pink rose heads on the lawn each time it rained. And unlike McDonough, where everything was a half hour drive in traffic, in Forest Park we could walk to the library, the park, the pool, and the MARTA bus route. Plus a Chick-fil-A, the Jamaican House of Curry, and a decent taqueria.

Jason built a pine bookshelf that fit perfectly in our new hallway. He bought our first lawnmower at the old Ace Hardware on Main Street.

He was busy painting the kitchen "Granny Smith" green when he got the phone call that he had been hired at a video production shop on the north side of Atlanta. We cheered in the half-painted room. Our center of gravity was shifting back towards the city; it finally felt like we were headed in the right direction.

Where else could you get all this for $650 a month? Of course it was cheap. The whole neighborhood smelled like jet fuel.

"Tell me something about Forest Park," said Dawn. "And please don't think I'm being racist. Why is it that when black people moved into the area, things went downhill so fast?"

She asked me this quietly, sincerely, as if I, at age twenty-five, would have some kind of wisdom. I felt like a contestant in a beauty pageant, the heat rising in my cheeks, but searching for the diplomatic response. I started to formulate an answer about the river of wealth it takes, constantly flowing through a community, to keep businesses busy, the lawns mowed and the sidewalks swept, the kids in good schools and parents in nice cars. That when the river is diverted, even a tiny bit, the ensuing drought reveals the riverbed, scarred and jumbled. There's a pattern of airport-impacted neighborhoods becoming low-income neighborhoods.

Instead, I said something about how it's not the race of the newcomers that matters, but the income level, the ability to commit and invest. And that for most of Atlanta's history, race and wealth have gone hand in hand. She didn't look very convinced. I am still working on my answer to Dawn's question.

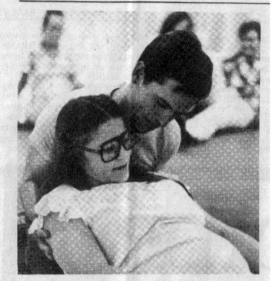

(Staff Photo By Don Renfroe)

JESSE AND JAYNE SLAGLE PERFORM EXERCISE
Mountain View Couple Is Taking Soromundi Course

The Clayton Neighbor, August 1976.

FIVE

THE BREAKUP

During our move from McDonough to Forest Park, the second move in only a few months, I found a box of photos and postcards given to me by my Granny. Inside was a newspaper clipping from *The Clayton Neighbor* from August 1976. Beneath the headline, "Natural Childbirth: Moms and Dads Stick Together in Clayton Delivery Rooms," there was a photo of my parents. My dad, smooth and earnest, supported his reclining wife. My mother's arms were plump in her ruffled peasant blouse. Her eyeglasses and belly were extravagantly round. The caption said, "Jesse and Jayne Slagle Perform Exercise. Mountain View Couple is Taking Soromundi Course."

"Natural childbirth" was newsworthy at that time, and fathers in the delivery room were still a novel sight. I was startled to see my parents together and embracing. They've been divorced as long as I can remember. Plus, they looked so young, and so much younger than I was at the time. But it wasn't the photo that got lodged in my head. It was the caption, "Mountain View Couple." I read it over and over. They were a couple; a couple from Mountain View. I studied how the letterforms bled into the fiber of the old newsprint. I was aware that Mountain View used to be a place and that my family lived there when I was born. But my parents broke up and the city had been wiped off the map and it was never clear to me how all this happened and when.

This is what makes moving so hard. Unearthing the lightest things.

DURING THAT FIRST SPRING back in Georgia, Jason and I made a number of expeditions into Mountain View, or what used to be Mountain View. As we drove slowly down Old Dixie Highway, we could spot overgrown patches of a street grid hidden in the dead space buffering the airport. I had heard that the entire city was "bought out," in the late 1970s, by whom exactly, I did not know. Located just east of the runways, Mountain View was a city in Clayton County that grew up alongside the airport. As we picked our way down old driveways that dried up in vacant lots, we were constantly yelling over the sound of cicadas or descending jets.

One of our biggest "discoveries" that day was an abandoned two-story office building in the middle of a forest. We left our car among a yard of junk cars at the amputated end of a road. A fence blocking the street was choked with honeysuckle. We found a body-sized puncture in the chain link and hiked up the wide path of retreating asphalt. Kudzu was overtaking everything.

The dilapidated building looked like it had been built in the late 1960s—wide horizontal planes of dark brick wrapped with a second story balcony. We didn't have to debate whether we should sneak in. Jason crept ahead of me, on the lookout for squatters. We stepped over toppled chairs and rain-warped debris to read a large map of Atlanta that was still tacked to the wood-paneled walls. A desk was littered with notepads bearing the logo of Estes Heating & Air, an Atlanta business that grew up in Mountain View. One rotary phone lay in the corner, as though there had been an emergency evacuation in the night.

Where there were signs of life, Mountain View resembled a post-apocalyptic settlement. Outside, we stopped to collect blackberries growing up through an old cement truck seized with rust. A man emerged from a hidden trailer and lumbered down the hill towards us. He was wearing one-piece coveralls unzipped to his furry navel. It turns out those were his blackberries and this was his land. It also turns out that he went to Forest Park High School with my father, and how is he by the way? Tell him Ricky Brownlee said hello.

Our conversation was muffled by an approaching jet. I looked up to read the underbelly of a Delta, its feet outstretched for landing. Jason took my hand and tugged me back toward the highway and we mouthed our goodbyes.

Who were these holdouts? Were they even allowed to live here anymore? And why was it called Mountain View? At that time, I could find nothing about Mountain View on the Internet. There was nothing on the maps. On the tracks that parallel Old Dixie Highway there was still a small railroad marker stamped MOUNTAIN VIEW. The spot seems to be elevated, but not exactly mountainous. Was it a mountain long ago? Did they chop off the hilltop and convert it to fill dirt for a runway?

Over time, I compiled my own answers to these questions based on scraps of hearsay and myth. In my working version of events, my family was forced out of Mountain View by heartless airport officials. We were evicted from our home, which was a charming Victorian at 133 South West Street. I imagined the old dame, hoisted out of her foundation onto a flatbed, draped in solemn Wide Load banners, and paraded down Old Dixie Highway.

I believe my house was tall and white. Maybe gray. The paint job was probably flaking. Definitely there was a concrete stoop. I don't know. I was only three when we left. Memories of the place are easily confused with old photos I've seen—the linoleum in the kitchen, matching cups on the countertop, a swing set in the damp backyard, and a hog in a pen.

It's possible that my version of events is entirely fictional. There are some questions that seem so fundamental, you feel that they must have been answered when you weren't paying attention. Or that the answers are so obvious, you are a fool for not figuring them out already. After enough years have passed, assumptions harden and you can't bring it up again. It would be impossibly rude, like asking your date, after the movie and dinner and dessert, emboldened by a few beers and tentative necking, I'm sorry, but can you tell me your name again?

What happened to my parents? And what happened to our house at 133 South West Street?

"THAT WAS A BEAUTIFUL OLD neighborhood," said my dad, who had migrated away from the airport, but still lived nearby. "I'll be driving sometimes and pass by South West Street and feel a kind of pang."

He went on to qualify this statement. "But the same thing happened to my parents in the '50s. The house they rented on Bell Street in College Park. It's all under the terminal now."

When my mother visited from Tennessee, I asked her to lead me to me the site of our first house at 133 South West Street. I was surprised that she agreed.

The old driveways were faintly marked by mailbox posts and leggy crepe myrtles.

Mom looked around wistfully, but never lost her trademark pep. She located a giant oak tree, shrouded in kudzu, that would have been in our front yard. We debated the orientation of the house. She turned around in the empty, weed-bitten street and shrugged. I kept waiting for some sight or smell to trigger the whole scene for me, but the landscape was completely effaced. A vast, neighboring plot was being cleared and graded for new construction. Just beyond that, I-75 roared like a waterfall.

She was blunt.

"It was cheap. We paid something like $250 a month for a three-bedroom."

They didn't own the place. As renters, they got $7,000 to relocate, which seems like a lot for 1980. Then she added, quite pleased with herself, "That's the money I used to move out on my own."

She did remember the name of the landlady, which I noted and later carried down to Jonesboro, home of *Gone With the Wind* and all the deed books in Clayton County history.

"ARE YOU SURE THAT'S the address?" asked the lady at the Tax Commissioner's office.

"Mountain View? What mountain?" said the lady at the Deeds and Records office.

Hoisting those oversized, leather-bound books of maps had the effect of making me feel small and maybe shrinking. I needed both hands to turn the giant pages. I could find no 133 South West Street. There was no South West Street at all. Where I remember the house being situated, there were only huge, blank parcels owned by development groups like TMT Holdings, and Highwoods Realty.

Yes, I'm sure that's the address. I was taught to memorize it in singsong rhyme, just in case I was ever kidnapped or lost.

Working my way back in time, I finally spotted the owner's name—Tammie Joe Davis—written on a tax map from 1985. It was hard to find because her name and all the others on the map had been crossed out in pencil and marked VOID. This is one way a house can die, when its "parcel" is absorbed into a larger property.

Tammie Joe sold her property to the City of Atlanta on September 30, 1981. When I finally located the description typewritten on a deed, it was like the distinct thrill of reading my own birth certificate:

Land Lot 12 of the 13th District of Clayton County Georgia, being Block "B" of the D.M. Harrison subdivision. Being improved property having located

thereon a one-story frame dwelling known as No. 133, formerly 174 South West
Street.

The documents got more and more ornate as I leapt back through
the deed books. The handwritten pages from 1901, when the original subdivision was created, were a tight lacework of diagonal scrawl.
The hand-drawn plat showed twenty-four deep city plots. My house
was just one parcel in a huge grid, one of a thousand Mountain View
houses in the flight path.

While it's possible to track down the history of the land, finding
the actual house is like trying to find a body. What did the City of
Atlanta do with all those perfectly good houses? Sold them in batches
to house movers, who auctioned them off to developers and bar-
gain-hunters with a plot of land. When I was a kid, seeing a house on
wheels, flanked by pilot trucks and creeping down the highway, was
not uncommon.

In Clayton County, Roy Bishop House Movers was the only
name in the game. While Bishop's name was on the business, the
prime mover, pun intended, was his business partner Ed Echols, a
Clayton County Commissioner. Since the days of relocating neighborhoods wholesale from the flight paths, the house moving business
has diminished to a niche market for relocating historic properties.
I reached out to the current owner of the company by phone. John
Kinard, a longtime veteran of the business, remembered clearing out
the neighborhoods of Mountain View in the early '80s.

He described how when his crew tried to move the first house out
on a trailer, protestors lay down across Old Dixie Highway to block
the convoy.

"I drug my share of houses out of there," he said. "At least three
hundred of them."

It would have been a scandal that these Mountain View holdouts
wished to stand, or lie down, in the way of progress. It seemed like
a controversy that I should be able to find chronicled in the local

newspapers. But I could find no documentation of the protests. The majority of Mountain View residents took their relocation checks, moved away, and didn't look back.

By the end of 1981, they must have moved my house. Or Tammie Joe's house. By then, I guess it was the City of Atlanta's house. I don't know what city it's in now.

I STARTED MY SEARCH FOR a new job by making a photocopy of the Yellow Pages page for "Printers." I made this copy, of course, at Bellamy Printing, along with a stack of my resumes. I even designed and printed thank-you cards to send to future employers. The dry spring days provided lots of golf time for Tommy. Sheryl pulled the office phone over to the open roll-form doors and smoked.

My commute from Forest Park to McDonough was forty-five minutes on a good day. I had been called into Tommy's office more than once and reprimanded for clocking in later than 7:30 am. Some mornings I got up extra early and drove to print shops close to our new house in Forest Park. ASAP Printing. Arrowhead Printing. Buddy's Blueprints. Crown Printing. All the way down the alphabet to TransWorld Printing. I was always certain to mention my maiden name, just in case it might have some currency.

One clear, hot morning, traveling down Old Dixie Highway between Geographics and Minuteman Printing, I saw the "mountain view." Stone Mountain is a geological oddity, a bulging granite "monadnock" twenty miles away. But here, momentarily, it was visible on the horizon, a steel blue dome swelling up through striated smog. I gasped and swerved. Atlanta is a sprawling place with very few such vistas, so this was like spotting a rainbow. I wanted to wave at other commuters and make them pull over with me to get a better look.

Mountain View Post Office Building, 2009.

SIX

TWO MAYORS

Mountain View's disappearance was a uniquely odd moment in Georgia's history. What did it take to revoke a city's charter and remove it from the map? I collected a list of terms referring to what had happened to the city: it was "erased," "dissolved," "dismantled," "devoured by suburbia." The residents "fled," were "forced out," and "abandoned the city." A sidebar in the Clayton News Daily reported that the city charter was revoked "as a way of cleaning up what had become the state's most wide-open town."

Wide-open? I had to zoom in on the microfiche and reread that. That's the first time I had encountered that term. Clearly no one knew what to call this event—the death of a city— because it had never happened before.

Jason and I got my father and stepmother talking about Mountain View over dinner one night. Our double dates were often storytelling sessions. Two Forest Park natives, both born in the 1950s, Dad and Gayle have been married long enough that they are starting to look like cousins. He wears suspenders and bowler hats; she has a necklace for every outfit. They deal out their memories on the table like a game of cards.

Dad said Mountain View's demise was the mayor's fault. The Mayor of Mountain View was Ray King, and my father summarized him as a "petty despot" whose political shiftiness was a frustration and embarrassment to the county commissioners. The sole elected official in Mountain View, the mayor "answered to no one. Except the senior citizens," Dad said. King took their phone calls and dispatched the free "Rapid Rabbit" transportation service to chauffeur them to the grocery store and doctor's office.

My father is not known for exaggeration. I found loads of bad press on King, who seemed to relish his image as an outlaw. He wore cowboy boots and carried a pistol. "I've been investigated by seven grand juries, three times by the IRS, four times by the FBI, and three times by the GBI," he bragged in the local paper. A high school dropout from east Tennessee, he was only thirty-two when elected mayor. During his four terms in office, King was charged with bribery, nepotism, conspiracy, assault, and violating the city charter by accepting an illegal salary.

Gayle suspected the Mountain View police department shared the blame for the loss of the city charter. The stretch of I-75 that passed through the city was a notorious speed trap. Locals knew that if you exceeded the speed limit by as little as two miles per hour, you got pulled over. Thousands of motorists passing through the state were ticketed.

In 1972, then-Governor Jimmy Carter suspended Mountain View's police powers for several months during an investigation into the alleged speed trap. Though no wrongdoing was confirmed, the allegations contributed to Mountain View's bad reputation. A defiant sign posted at the north end of the city said: WELCOME TO MOUNTAIN VIEW. WE HOPE YOU LOVE YOUR DRIVER'S LICENSE AS MUCH AS WE LOVE OUR CHILDREN.

And then there was the booze. Shortly after taking office, King authorized the sale of alcohol in an otherwise dry county. Residents of Mountain View paid no city tax thanks to the revenue from their

nickel-a-can tax on beer. Package stores like Charlie's Market, The
Yellow Jacket Market, and The Jet Stop Market were busy twenty-four
hours a day, except Sundays. King claimed that they didn't even have
locks on the doors. My dad remembered a towering display in the
front of Charlie's Market for Polly Peachtree Shaving Lotion, a cheap,
"barely potable fruit liqueur, popular with the under-the-bridge set."
It was made in Atlanta.

Mountain View's reputation for rowdy taverns and nightclubs,
public drunkenness and fighting were an offense to the people of
Clayton County. In 1976, a delegation of five county legislators proposed a bill in the Georgia General Assembly to abolish the city
charter, calling Mountain View "a blight on Clayton County." State
Representative Rudolph Johnson of Morrow, chair of the delegation,
employed a scattershot approach: "They've had controversy out
there for twenty years. It's an accumulation of things, really."

So was it Mayberry or the Wild West? Whenever I asked friends
or family who remembered, they all suggested that the city had it
coming.

"Well, you know what happened to Mountain View," they'd say.

"What?"

"That crooked mayor," or "The chief of police was corrupt," or
"They had to clean up that whole area, it was so wide-open."

"So they bulldozed the whole city because of the mayor?" I asked.
"Because of liquor stores? Why didn't they hold a special election? Why didn't they just get a new mayor, or clean up the police
department?"

No one knew. Another lost cause.

They believed these scandals were reason enough to repeal a city
charter. In January 1978, the city of Mountain View, "The Gateway to
Clayton County," population 3,000, ceased to exist as a legal entity,
by a show of hands in the gold-domed state capital. Signing the bill,
Governor George Busbee called it a, "warning that abuse of the public trust will not be tolerated in Georgia."

Most shocking was that during the same month, King, the chief of police, and a Mountain View police officer were convicted of beating and conspiring to violate the civil rights of David Henry Anderson, a twenty-three year-old black man in their custody. A sloppy arrest turned violent because King, increasingly paranoid and combative, believed that Anderson was a hit man, hired by his political opponents. In his own defense, King said, "I feel any time the FBI sets out to get a politician, they either get assassinated or sentenced. I feel very fortunate to be sentenced instead of six feet under."

After a long and ugly battle, Mountain View finally shut down, its assets turned over to the state. King spent the next six years in a federal correctional facility in Lexington, Kentucky.

The prevailing narrative was that Mountain View, with its lax morals and corrupt mayor, was rightfully purged by the upright leaders of Clayton County.

But I'm skeptical.

Another young and ambitious mayor was part of the story. In 1973, Maynard Jackson Jr., age thirty-five, was elected mayor of Atlanta and became the first African-American mayor of a major Southern city. He took office at a time when Atlanta, like many American cities, had been gutted by white flight and was grappling with deep budget issues. Jackson served until he reached his term limit in 1982, and then was re-elected for another term from 1990-1994. The son of Atlanta's civil rights movement, Jackson's tenure as mayor guided Atlanta's transformation from a Southern crossroads to a major international city, home of the Olympic Games and the world's busiest airport. Jackson's legacy as mayor is reflected in the name of Hartsfield-Jackson Atlanta International Airport.

Jackson deserves credit for delivering on Hartsfield's moonshot of the 1960s, directing the complete reinvention of the airport, including the new Central Passenger Terminal and runway system that made the airport a dominant force in global aviation. In the process, Jackson instituted affirmative action programs that boosted minority participation in municipal contracts from less than 1 percent to more than 35 percent. That the Jackson administration built the airport on time and within budget, and with significant minority participation, both stymied Jackson's critics and fueled a generation of African-American business owners and civic leaders.

The deposed, white middle class could only look on from the suburbs at Jackson's monumental accomplishments and suspect corruption. The showdown between Mountain View Mayor Ray King and Atlanta Mayor Maynard Jackson was symbolic of the clash between two visions of the urban South. What used to be a constellation of rural, racially segregated hamlets was rapidly evolving into metropolitan Atlanta.

But it was the white officials before Jackson who set all this in motion. Hartsfield's all-white administration asserted a vision for a radically new southside, one with runways on top of neighborhoods. When did the city politicians realize how big this thing could be? And when did they start planning for the busiest airport in the world? I read the airport master plans that lead up to the celebrated grand opening of the 1980 terminal. The answer is, almost immediately after the first jets started traveling out of Atlanta in 1961. The airport had acquired and "converted" hundreds of homes in College Park and Hapeville to clear the way for airport facilities long before young Maynard Jackson had any political aspirations.

Jackson's administration was left to deal with the fallout of communities, mostly outside of his jurisdiction, who were living under the flight paths. In 1978, sound expert Dr. Clifford Bragdon called Mountain View the "most noise-impacted city in the U.S. or Europe." For a full decade before the airport had any official noise compatibility program, the Department of Aviation was systematically clearing out Mountain View and other flight path neighborhoods, not to build runways but to be "a good neighbor." Despite the constant roar of jet engines, many residents refused to sell, and their homes were taken by eminent domain.

In the fall of 1979, around the same time my parents were headed for divorce, Eastern Airlines created a special advertising section for *The Atlanta Journal*. Bold text floats over an illustration of a heavenly sunrise.

The clouds part to announce the good news: FLY INTO THE FUTURE: Only a few hundred yards from the old Atlanta Hartsfield terminal, through which millions have passed, a totally new passenger facility will handle its first flight. It will be the largest terminal in the world, the product of years of planning, hundreds of millions of dollars, and a vision of the future of air travel.

A full-color spread illustrates the $100 million new terminal from overhead. Four wide concourses are planted where a hundred cartoon jets point to their gates. The surrounding airport area is sketched in as an even expanse of fluffy trees. Beyond that is a clear blank. In advertising, it's called copy space. But any Atlanta native would know that the blank space is occupied by established neighborhoods. The airport wasn't built on blank woodlands. I knew it was built on top of cities like College Park and Hapeville, and—at least up until 1978—Mountain View.

In that same issue celebrating the airport's success, an interviewer asked Jackson if he would have done anything differently. He answered:

"Hindsight is always a great help in detecting problems. There are several things I would have done. One would be to work closely with the local jurisdictions on zoning, limiting development around the airport to industrial areas with no residential build-up. Also, we would have worked to resolve the potential difficulty with Clayton County a long time ago. Years ago, I would have attempted to annex into Atlanta the entire airport reservation...all of this would have been completed before the new terminal was built."

This was the first and only instance I found where Jackson addresses the conflict between the adjacent communities and the massive airport that now bears his name. I solemnly highlighted the passage like scripture, seeing holy land reduced to "residential build-up" and listed among the great leader's regrets.

That statement was also a subtle criticism of previous planners and leaders, like mayors Hartsfield and Ivan Allen Jr., who directed significant investment into Atlanta's aviation assets, but failed to head off the "difficulty with Clayton County" and prevent developers from building thousands of homes around the growing airport. Homes that would have to be acquired, neighborhood by neighborhood, and replaced with noise-compatible uses.

How CAN I EXPLAIN WHY Mayor Ray King was so deeply admired by his constituents? When he died in 2004, he was eulogized by former Mountain View residents for fighting for their community, providing the neighborhood kids with a ballpark, a swimming pool, and baseball uniforms. He gets credit for extending city services such as free garbage pick-up, police and fire protection to Plunkett Town, the poor, black settlement separated from Mountain View by the county line, the railroad, and a grassy field.

"I'm not a crook," he said. "I'm just a country boy with a tenth grade education. I've got kids of my own and I want them to grow up here in Mountain View."

He was known for staging protests against the airport. He accused Clayton County legislators of "banding together with real estate interests who want to make Mountain View an industrial area."

How soon did he know that his city's very existence was negotiable? I can see how he was an embarrassment and a threat to the airport-boostering county commissioners. I can see how the battle made him paranoid, left him swinging as the world became unrecognizable to him.

I heard that King got in trouble for floating huge weather balloons in the flight path. That's how close the planes were flying—that a balloon-wielding man could be a symbol of resistance.

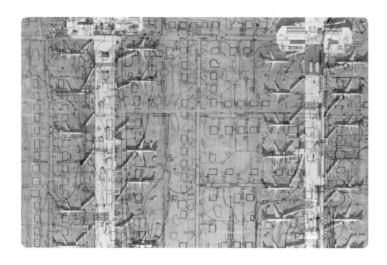

1967 Airport area map layered with satellite view of H-JAIA terminals.

SEVEN

BIRD'S EYE VIEW

Friday, March 11, 2005. An inmate being escorted to a holding cell in the Fulton County Justice Tower on Central Avenue assaulted a sheriff's deputy and pocketed her Beretta semi-automatic. After locking the deputy in a cell and changing into street clothes, the inmate crossed into the Fulton County Courthouse via sky bridge. The inmate hunted down his trial judge, whom he shot at point-blank range as the judge sat on the bench, along with the court reporter and, moments later, the sergeant who pursued him down seven flights of stairs, out an emergency exit, into the morning rush hour traffic on Martin Luther King Jr. Drive. The mayhem continued with five car-jackings at gunpoint, through a series of downtown parking decks, each advancing the assailant a few blocks north on Peachtree Street, north on Spring Street, over to CNN Center, and back to the Five Points MARTA Station where, on foot, his trail disappeared by 9:20 AM.

I followed the manhunt for Brian Nichols in real time from my desk at my new typesetting job at Minuteman Printing. I was bored.

Most mornings, my job consisted of updating the room service menus for Hilton Hotels and Hilton Garden Inns. I liked to announce the most egregious prices to my cubicle mates—$10.95 for scrambled eggs, $16.95 for a waffle. Minuteman Printing was a founding member of the Airport Area Chamber of Commerce, and our main customers were AirTran, Delta, and the dozens of hotels, restaurants, event facilities, and conference centers that fed off the airport.

But right now, Nichols' disturbingly handsome mugshot covered my screen. For once, Atlanta was at the top of the national news; we had captured the headlines on all the Internet news sites. All morning the city was on lockdown as the search continued. A swarm of helicopters clustered over downtown and broadcast the view of the roadblocks below. I watched these aerial scenes streaming live online.

I had recently been reprimanded for "abusing your Internet privileges." My supervisor, Deb, a member of the family that owned the print shop, blushed painfully as she explained the gravity of this misconduct. The original founders of Minuteman Printing had retired and left the daily print shop operations to their children, now in late middle age.

"They have programs where they can check what sites you've been visiting," she warned. I nodded and tried to look serious, but this seemed silly, like a teacher criticizing a student for spending too much time in the library. Where else was I supposed to find examples of good graphic design? Not in Hapeville. To me, "reading" the Internet was more than an educational time-waster, it was as compulsive as breathing. It was one of the few tradeoffs for agreeing to spend my twenties stationed at a computer for 8.5 hours a day. At my first desk job out of college in New York City, the startup culture promoted web-surfing as a competitive sport. The whole island vibrated with newsworthy innovation and drama, every nuance of which was breathlessly reported online. And now, instead of being in the center of the media universe, I was experiencing current events from a cheap, rolling task chair in a windowless corner of a print shop by the Atlanta airport.

I doubted my own ability to "quit" the Internet. Still, Deb had a kind, maternal appeal and I wanted to please her. She sat directly behind me and could see my computer screen. It's not like I snuck over to Yahoo. com while Hilton menus were waiting to be updated. I struggled to make myself unimpeachable. Jason and I were trying to buy a house back then and I needed some kind of job history to get a mortgage.

The room where I worked was divided into four fluorescent-lit stations. Deb managed an entire quadrant with two computer stations and a reef of color-coded work orders. I shared another corner with Pauline, a boisterous, fifty-something cat lady and my new "Dawn" at work. She generously taught me some neat Photoshop tricks and let me come over to her place after work to lie in her tanning bed.

Pauline was a lifelong resident of "Happy-ville," as she called it, a triangular city formed by interstates I-75 and I-85 where they merge into the fourteen-lane behemoth known to Atlanta commuters as "The Connector." At the base of this triangle lies Hartsfield-Jackson Atlanta International Airport, a bustling grayfield surrounded by bushy green. The Norfolk Southern Railroad stitched up the long belly of Central Avenue, where Minuteman, the original Chick-fil-A, and the Ford assembly plant were located. I had the sense that the city was a thin slice; it could not expand. That the transportation corridors on all sides were a kind of moat that both protected and trapped its residents.

During my six-month tenure at Minuteman Printing, I witnessed such historic events as the "swift-boating" of the 2004 presidential election and the Indonesian tsunami that followed right after Christmas. The hunt for Nichols had us all in a tizzy. Until he resurfaced the next morning at a suburban apartment complex in Duluth, Georgia, it seemed as though he could show up anywhere, at any time, and kill us all.

When I say that I "followed" him online, I mean I traced his steps by clicking around the flesh-colored map of downtown Atlanta on MapQuest.com. Central Avenue to MLK Drive, Peachtree to Spring Street, Underground Atlanta to CNN Center.

I remember this clearly because Deb was walking past by my work station and caught me in the act. Maybe it was the festival atmosphere of the courthouse mayhem, but instead of scolding me, she said, "You know, it's easier with Google Maps."

I did not know, so she showed me. Rather than clicking on one of the cardinal directions and waiting for the next square mile to load on your screen, you could, for the first time, click, grab, and drag the map in any direction. The navigation was fluid, instant, and addictive. This may sound like a minor advancement, but it was so astonishing that I distinctly remember using it for the first time. Launched just a month earlier, in February 2005, Google Maps quickly dominated digital mapping, making converts of every level of user from expert cartographers to the Sales and Prepress departments of Minuteman Printing in Hapeville, Georgia. I now view the launch of Google Maps as equally historic to the re-election of George W. Bush or the great tsunami, and more revolutionary. Nichols, who later became Georgia's most expensive defendant of all time, is only memorable to me because of the maps.

Surely we relied on Internet maps before Google Maps came along. That winter Jason and I drained a number of ink cartridges by printing dozens of them as we scoured Forest Park, Hapeville, and East Point for a house under $110,000. We searched these neighborhoods because the southside was our home territory, and we assumed it was still affordable. But even crappy two bedroom houses with house jacks in the basement holding up the cracked foundation, or houses sharing a driveway with a Church's Fried Chicken, or those penetrated by fleas, reeking of motor oil or cat piss—even these houses were out of our range. Shopping for a house in 2005 was a brutal lesson in real estate heartbreak. We were pained by how little we could afford and unprepared for the bidding wars. Our offers fell through on three different properties, and each loss was a kind of minor miscarriage. I recall an enormous cell phone bill composed of back-and-forth calls to the mortgage banker and quite a bit of face-down crying on the futon as our lease expired.

When we finally spotted a contender in East Point, Jason and I were determined not to let it get away. It met all our criteria for a modest dream home—a solid 1940s cottage with a fenced backyard and two outbuildings for studio space—and was listed at $140,000.

What did we know about East Point? Only that it was one of those old Atlanta suburbs, a couple miles north of the airport, that used to be white and was now black. It was part of that mysterious swath of the southside that we circumvented on interstate highways, an inner ring of the city that was mentioned only in vague warnings and hip hop lyrics. There were pockets of beautifully preserved historic homes in East Point, but we couldn't afford those houses, either. We were shopping on the edge of a questionable part of town. But it was midway between our jobs in the city and our family in the outer suburbs.

Our real estate agent was a big fan. He chauffeured us around a small Southern town that had its own quaint Main Street district and MARTA train station, easy access to downtown, low property taxes, and lots of charming, cheap old houses on wide and quiet streets. Jason and I were somewhat emboldened by the fact that our grandparents had East Point roots—my dad's dad worked at the Prestolite Battery Plant for decades, Gayle's father graduated from Russell High, and Mom's parents owned a bake shop on Stewart Avenue in the 1960s. Despite these connections, our families were skeptical about our plans to move there.

"You need to think about the schools," they warned.

We laughed. "We don't even have kids!"

One weekend after Christmas, an ice storm immobilized all of Atlanta, so Jason and I seized the opportunity to outwit more timid house hunters. I had a custom Google map in my lap that directed us from Forest Park to East Point via Norman Berry Avenue. We rolled slowly down the deserted boulevard, feeling like the only house hunters in the world. The pear trees, enrobed in ice, locked with the wilted pines to form a glazed arbor over the road. This was my first impression of our neighborhood.

My few months at Minuteman, even if I was making only $12 an hour, were enough to establish employment to get a mortgage. The morning we closed on the house I was so nervous, caffeinated, or both, I sliced the tip of my left index finger with an Xacto blade. Drops of blood landed on the paste-up board and the smell of warm wax made me feel woozy.

I showed Deb my bloody wad of paper towels and she dispatched me to the clinic next door to get stitches. I had visited the clinic a few weeks prior for the first and only drug test of my life. It was humiliating. I signed all the closing papers with a corndog-shaped bandage on my finger.

For years we used digital maps the same way we used the Rand-McNally Atlas—for directions, mileage, and points of interest. But these new digital maps were different. Suddenly a map wasn't a reference tool, but a virtual reality. In April 2005, Google satellite views went live, and I remember visiting the Eiffel Tower and the Pyramids of Giza from my desk in Hapeville. I was zooming in on the beaches of Florida for fun, examining my old neighborhood in Brooklyn for signs of familiarity. Even more exotic was the view of our new house from outer space. Someone else's car sat in the miniature driveway. It didn't look like our house yet.

It was like the airport blueprints from Bellamy Printing, only better. With Satellite Views, I could see, in great detail, what the pilots saw as they maneuvered into this airspace. Like an air traveler, I could see Hapeville's sullen rooftops and winking streetlights. Private yards laid bare for porthole gazers: an inflatable kiddie pool in a cinder block courtyard; a circle of dirt carved by an animal on a chain. Backyard mimosa trees spilling over the tops of the interstate walls.

This is what developers saw when they looked down on the southside and planned new runways and buyouts. This is what the legendary urban theorist Jane Jacobs called the planners' "Olympian" view.

But Google Maps wasn't yet able to document what I longed to see—the past. It would be years before I was able to overlay historic maps of the airport with current satellite images to see the landscape before and after. A 1967 map of the airport, found in the archives of Georgia State University, showed me the scale of displacement. Thousands of houses, tiny square boxes, from College Park to Mountain View, dotted the area that would become the modern airport reservation. To toggle between maps is breathtaking, even if you didn't grow up there with the hunted feeling that your past had been erased. It's like finding evidence of a whole part of your life that you thought had been completely wiped out.

From my seat at Minuteman I looked for my old house in Mountain View. The street map showed South West Street as a short alleyway that dead-ended into a parking lot. But the satellite map had not fully registered these revisions. The overhead map included the ghostly path of my old street overlaying a crisp asphalt parking lot. I saved a screenshot of the mistake. Eventually, Google Maps will correct it and erase my old block entirely.

King/Goss residence, Mountain View, 2009.

EIGHT

WALKING TOURS OF LOST CITIES

We met like spies in broad daylight. The Stovalls, unofficial ambassadors of Mountain View, arranged to find Jason and me in the parking lot of a doughnut shop on Old Dixie Highway, the only landmark we both recognized on an otherwise foreign strip. Jason would take photos; I would take notes. We promised to arrive in a black sedan, they would be in a white SUV. I smiled about these plans when I realized theirs was the only car in sight. It was a Sunday in late July and the ninety-degree high guaranteed us a heat-enforced ghost town.

Blanchard's Bakery, one of the few businesses left in the area formerly known as Mountain View, was closed. Everyone had retreated to a patch of AC. Air traffic, on the other hand, was brisk. Every three minutes or so a plane dipped into the frame of my windshield, drawing the dry treetops in its glittering wake. I watched them descend over the bulbous Clayton County Water Authority tower, past long rows of warehouses, past the jungly, abandoned neighborhoods of Mountain View, over ten lanes of I-75, to the horizon where it attached to the tarmac. The Stovalls were waiting for us when we arrived.

Jason and I dashed from our car to theirs. The momentary blast of jet noise and heat were like a hair dryer to the face.

As we slid across the leather back seat of their Mountaineer, Rusty and Debbie twisted around to greet us. They'd been watching the planes for a few minutes. Sometimes two or even three would descend almost simultaneously. We all smiled nervously and agreed that this place was unlivable.

I set up this meeting with the Stovalls after having dinner with an old high school friend named Jamie. Both of us had recently moved to East Point, so we talked about the neighborhood, the state of the southside, the airport, all the people who had come and gone. She put me in touch with her in-laws, who were natives of Mountain View. Jamie emailed Mrs. Stovall's contact information with a note that said, "Just remind her that you were once Slagle and she should remember who you are! I'm thinking of you and Jason and praying for you both."

It wasn't hard to find people with stories about Mountain View. Everybody I know has an aunt or a father-in-law who lived there, who worked for Delta or Eastern back in the old days. They lived in Mountain View, Forest Park, and Hapeville in the days before the airport grew into their backyards. They are often burning with stories—some nostalgic, some laced with conspiracy theories, most just longing for confirmation that Mountain View was real and not a fluke of memory.

The Stovalls were my parents' age, but had the names of kids. Debbie wore pressed white shorts and a neat blond bob. Rusty had changed from his church clothes into a red polo buckled into blue jeans. They were high school sweethearts. Now that their sons were grown and had children of their own, they bantered like a slightly gray version of their high school selves. They couldn't believe we wanted to go on this tour, but they obliged us politely.

Rusty and Debbie Stovall grew up in the city of Mountain View during the brief and tumultuous years of its existence. Their childhood and teenage years coincided neatly with the city's stunted adolescence. The city was incorporated in 1949, and lost its charter in

1978. Debbie's family relocated southward in 1961; Rusty's held out a few years more. They were married in 1974 at Mountain View Baptist Church. So accelerated was the lifespan of this southside neighborhood that a single generation can encapsulate the city's history in its entirety.

Debbie had a yellowish stack of newspaper clippings and photos in her lap. They described a small town where everyone was related. "That's how we ended up with 350 people at our wedding," she joked.

One large-format shot showed the congregation of Mountain View Baptist posing in front of the church. Behind the crowd, a residential street angled off into the distance. It resembled any of the great old neighborhoods in Atlanta—Virginia-Highland or Morningside or Capitol View. Late '50s cars and trucks, glossy black, were parked in front of the rows of neat, brick bungalows.

"This is half the town," said Debbie. "We know everybody in this photo."

As we began our driving tour of the city—or the few blocks that used to constitute the city—I scribbled down these stories while Jason kept the Stovalls talking. Rusty retained a young boy's fascination for the macabre. He pointed out the spot on The Nancy Hanks Line where a train going sixty miles an hour hit a '59 Chevy and wrapped it around the cowcatcher, killing two. He gestured towards the field where the Kinsler twins, a boy and a girl, suffocated after climbing into an old chest freezer.

Debbie remembered the characters from church, where her father was the music director for twenty-five years.

"Everything took place either at the school or at the church," she said.

Something reminded her of Mr. Lee, the eccentric old man who came to church wearing wild, flower print neckties only to sleep through the service. Maybe we passed the site of his house. Rusty slowed by the spot where Mountain View Baptist used to stand. It was just a wooded hill between the water tower and a parking lot.

"When they tore it down, everybody went in there and grabbed a brick," she told me. "They saved the stained glass, everything."

I pictured a festive scene. Men, women, and kids, picking through heaps of colored glass and brick. Inside the car, the air conditioner whined.

Rusty showed us the site of Mountain View Elementary across the street. I saw nothing more than an overgrown fence. An orange sofa slouched beneath a sign that said, "No Dumping. $1000 Fine." I wondered if the Stovalls would mind if Jason and I climbed the fence.

I was tempted to wade into the sweet kudzu and search for skeletal remains of our house—the foundation, curbs, or the concrete stoop. I glanced from my pink ankles to the lumpy greenery and imagined hazards just beneath the surface—dumped and severed pipe, shards of scrap fencing, animal decay, and West Nile virus.

With the Stovalls, I was drawn to the site of my old home like a bonfire. It had become the backside of a shining Federal Aviation Administration complex. Rusty and Debbie were casually looking for evidence of the church, but I got out of the car. Beyond the chain-link fence at the end of South West Street lay a fresh black parking lot surrounded by spiked iron fencing. So this was the site of my old house, the faint street line still marked on Google Maps. A leathery security guard eyed us from his booth. The ground was so hot, the asphalt seemed to be coming unglued under my feet. I was holding my breath for some reason.

BACK IN THE CAR, we headed north. Rusty was peering through the windshield, studying Old Dixie for the former turnoff of his street, Morris Street. To our right was a steep bank of granite gravel topped with railroad tracks, to the left, a winding complex of commercial warehouses named "Atlanta Tradeport." Again the crepe myrtles, whose sole landscaping function is to demarcate property lines, bordered the planted pines. Their shaggy pink tops swept the air.

"The noise really started in the early '60s," Rusty said, "Before that, it was all prop planes. We were directly underneath. I could see the people in the windows of the planes." He showed me the boundaries of Plunkett Town, the black side of town, where the buyouts began.

"In the early '70s they came and bought the air rights across the street. They topped the pine trees—that's how low the planes were coming in."

One neighbor protested by mounting a flagpole tall enough to interfere with the airspace. He flew the American flag upside down.

"We've passed it," Rusty said.

We pulled into the Tradeport maze and looped through the parking lot. Satair, Siemens, and FedEx all have vast square footage in the nameless complex. We turned south again, and I felt the beginnings of carsickness. I stopped writing and gazed straight ahead at the road. The storefronts we passed were a mix of holdouts and newcomers— AA Used Appliance, Catalina Super Market, and Sosebee's Wrecker Service. The Stovalls narrated the old tenants—Whitmeyer's General Store, the GEX, the depot. But where was Morris Street?

"It's really okay if you can't find it," I offered. Rusty was determined. We looked for the county line.

"It was at the top of the hill. You had to cross it to buy firecrackers," said Debbie.

The hill itself seemed to be gone.

"I don't recognize any of this," he muttered. "These streets don't relate to anything now."

"Can you see Stone Mountain from here?" I piped up from the backseat.

Rusty was scanning both sides of the street, driving at a crawl.

"There it is, look."

"Where?"

"Just there, you can barely see it."

We all studied the eastern horizon.

"That's a landfill," said Jason.

Resigned, Mr. Stovall crossed the tracks to show us the old post office. The sign in front of the small, white cinder block building said, BELIEVERS WALKING IN THE WAY OF RIGHTEOUSNESS. Service times were listed below.

Debbie handed me a faded photo of the same perfectly symmetrical building where the sign said: MOUNTAIN VIEW, GA 30070. Her cousin, the postmaster, redheaded, horn-rimmed, and uniformed, stood proudly by the front door with his arms crossed. Even a postage stamp-sized post office puts a city indisputably on the map.

Rusty eased into the shattered driveway of a house, one of the only remaining residential structures in Mountain View. We'd driven past it several times in the last hour and only just noticed it behind the trees.

Debbie recognized it slowly. "This is Mrs. Goss's house," she said. "She babysat for all the children from church."

We watched the house through the windshield, as if it might move. A red brick cottage with an arched doorway, it was well hidden behind a screen of privet and low tree limbs. The steep roof was rubbed raw in patches. Part of a white toilet stood where the driveway ended in debris.

At last Rusty shut off the engine and stepped out of the car. Jason and I followed, then Mrs. Stovall.

"She kept her hair in a bun. Do you remember how she used to plait it?" she asked. No one answered. We fanned out, stepping carefully through the tall weeds. I wondered who owned this place and if we were trespassing.

Rusty ambled down the driveway, appraising a commode that sat there. "Her son was the plumber. He took care of everyone's plumbing." He and Jason disappeared around back while I stepped onto the front porch.

I edged towards the windows and tried to peek inside the abandoned house. The wood casings had decayed, but the brick was still sturdy and red. I was feeling hopeful, picturing a location for the

Mountain View historical society. Just scrape off the roof and rent a
Bobcat to rip out the overgrowth. Swatting at the mosquitoes around
my shins, I kicked at the tall, tickling crab grass.

I turned back to Debbie and said, cheerfully, "We shouldn't have
worn shorts."

But she had not ventured towards the house. She was quietly
scooping tears away from her mascara.

"This is why I don't come back here," she said. "There is nothing
left of our childhood."

Hearing her apology, it occurred to me that Debbie must have
been one of the children Mrs. Goss watched. She might have spent a
few or a hundred afternoons playing on the cool floor of this house.
Of course, she would have marveled over the braids in this old lady's
hair in the same way I memorized my grandmother's hands as she
read to me. I used to trace the ridges of her fingernails and her cool,
translucent skin. Like Rusty's urban legends, these were the observations of a child. Homeless and crude, they came swarming up from
this patch of land. I braced myself for my own memories to descend,
but none came.

THE LAST HOUSE ON SOUTH WEST Street wasn't really a house
anymore. It was the headquarters and sole location of Dell Air, which
sounds like an airline, but is really a small heating and air conditioning shop founded by Dell Thompson. Not long after my tour with the
Stovalls, I went back to Mountain View to meet him.

"My dad bought this house when I was six months old," he told
me. "In 1942. Back then, it had an outhouse."

The house sat on the corner of Old Dixie Highway and South
West Street. It is the only original house left on a block that now ter-
minates at the iron gates of an FAA building.

It should be no surprise that I found a family connection to Dell
Thompson. My husband grew up with Dell's son because their moth-
ers were best friends. Now retired and living in Alabama, he met me at

the office during one of his visits to Atlanta for medical appointments. I told him my parents had lived on South West Street; it was my first home too.

The neighborhood of his childhood home sounds rural: chickens and goats, garden plots, a general store, and outhouses. Thompson lived there until 1960, the year he graduated from Forest Park High School. That's when his family moved out of Mountain View. Dell married, had kids, and came back in 1973 to set up his own business in the old house. He knew the location was ideal; he had learned the trade right down the street at his first job with Estes Heating & Air.

Thompson reminded me of that stoic uncle who's a fixture at every cookout and holiday, maintaining his quiet post. A tall man in his sixties with the heavy hands and shoulders of a blue-collar journeyman. Thompson's measured, quiet demeanor could be a form of shyness. Or maybe it was the natural reticence of any interviewee. He kept his hands in his pockets and directed his words not really to me, but to the spaces off to the side. He didn't have much to say, so I asked for a tour.

The house had survived many conversions and additions over the years. The bricked-in porch was converted to the company vault. A two-story addition off the back of the house more than doubled its square footage and gave the place a decidedly commercial entrance off Old Dixie Highway. This architectural hodgepodge was cemented, literally, by a wraparound parking lot that connected the office to a long storage warehouse.

Even so, the heart of Dell Air was a lovely old bungalow. For me, it was an obvious model for my lost house down the block.

Inside, the domestic touches gave me flutters. The arched doorways and heavy glass knobs. The glossy tile indicating an otherwise hidden fireplace. Look past the traffic jam of filing cabinets and a service map rudely stapled to the wall, and it wasn't difficult to imagine living there.

Except for the airplane noise. Because of the constant roar, business was conducted down the hall, in the unfortunately wood-paneled, but better-insulated addition to the office. The whole time we were talking, we were also lip reading. It's a skill, he joked, that was part of growing up in Mountain View.

I asked if he remembered when the airport noise started to become a problem.

"In the '40s, I guess," he said. "But before that it was the trains."

The Nancy Hanks Line, which ran mail for the U.S. Postal Service, was a regular presence in the neighborhood. The train came through every morning at 9:00 AM, made the trip to Macon, Savannah, and passed through again by 6:00 PM There were three railroad crossings in Mountain View, each one a dangerous intersection.

"The trains were always billowing black smoke," he said. "In the '50s, they tried to make the trains slow down."

He shook his head. Another lost cause. This was never a great place to live.

We stepped outside and I snapped some photos. He casually mentioned that the house was going to be torn down soon. He already had a deal with the county to sell the property; it was just a matter of timing.

I kept digging for some trace of sentimentality. Wasn't there anything about the place he would miss? Not really, he said, amused that I would suggest it.

Thompson was pragmatic, but he did show me one thing. We searched for the spot where the back stoop used to be. Where his father scratched his initials in the soft concrete. He kicked aside the clumped weeds to find it: D.T. E.T. '55. A small memorial, it was supposed to last forever.

NINE

RUN AWAY FROM HOME

My first runaway attempt was not a complete failure. I was on foot, traveling light, and quickly realized the limitations of my plan. I was four years old.

I announced my intentions over breakfast one Saturday morning. My sister, age six, sat across the table, tracing her name in a bowl of oatmeal: M-Y-R-A. Dad heard me from the kitchen.

"Today?" he asked.

"Yep."

"Where you headed?"

"It's a secret."

He wasn't angry. He offered to help me pack.

We filled a brown paper sack with my two favorite shirts and an apple. Myra hovered, interrogating. Dad wrote our phone number and address on a slip of paper and told me to keep in touch—110 Barnett Road, 363-4070. But I stalled. After supper, I finally started walking down the block. Between our house and Old Dixie Highway lay a trailer park on the left and Albert's junky machine shop on the right. I looked back to wave goodbye. My broken family stood by the mailbox, silhouetted by the amber sun. Dad was waving; my sister was sobbing. Though I could barely hear her, I could see her freckled face—scrunched up, howling.

I couldn't do it. I didn't have permission to cross streets by myself. I galloped back to them, laughing. "Don't cry," I said. "I was just playing."

This episode went down in family lore as an example of my independent streak and my father's liberal parenting. At least, that's how I liked to tell the story. My sister revised her version slightly. "I was crying because I wouldn't have anyone to pick on," she said.

It wasn't long before I fell in love with plucky runaways in books and TV shows. As a kid, I dreamed of leading a hidden tribe of orphans in the forest. At age four, however, I was too young for romantic plans. I was probably running after my mother.

Dad was the stable parent with the job at Superior Steel and the house on Barnett Road. Imagine his position—thirty years old, newly divorced, and moving two tiny daughters into this old house. Imagine your wife leaves and then your youngest child declares her intentions to run away from home. The child magnifies the hours of each day, observing everything. The thirty-year-old wants to fast forward through hard times, from the divorce to the next wedding. Whole years get swallowed up.

Family stories from this time are rife with trauma. The time I stepped in front of a heavy wooden swing and needed a half-dozen stitches in my forehead. The time I tumbled out of the babysitter's car as she was rounding the corner of South Avenue and Ash Street. The puppies that vanished after they got into rat poison. A different dog mistaken for a wolf and taken to the pound. The times we hid the green plastic comb Dad used to tug through our tangled wet hair. The time he tied a string from Myra's baby tooth to a doorknob and slammed the door. The string came loose, not the tooth. These stories are my only evidence that those years existed.

Two girls came over to our house, the daughters of a lady Dad was talking to. We gathered pecans and bashed them with a wooden mallet on the front stoop while our parents shared a beer. One of the sisters had seen the horror movie *Friday the 13th* and explained the scene where Jason emerges from the lake and pulls Alice from her canoe. Alarmed by this forbidden content, I ran inside to tell Dad. I jerked open the screen door to find another frightening scene on the porch: my father and his guest, deep in conversation. She had one knee draped over his and was laughing warmly at something he said.

Nothing much came of that conversation and those girls never visited again. But it was a warning not to get too comfortable in this place, with this family-of-three arrangement. At any moment, it could change.

I MEMORIZED THE TEXTURE OF the soil under the pecan tree, the smell of daffodils shooting up through dead leaves, and the best path, barefoot, between the gravel driveway and the rope swing. But I can't recall the exterior of the house. Was it painted green or was that the color of the light? I have never seen a photograph of the house, from the time we lived there. There aren't many images of me from age three to six, or my sister from five to eight. My father is the only one who knows about Barnett Road and I am loathe to ask him for details. I have bright and playful memories of the house, but those are years my dad would rather forget.

This lack of documentation means I know very little about the house or its history. I have a few fragments of information. First, that the property was owned by a friend who offered to let us stay there for free and my father spent a month cleaning and renovating to make it inhabitable, in the same way that Jason and I rehabilitated the "cabin" in McDonough. The owner might have been one of Dad's or Granddaddy's friends from church—our neighborhood was full of helpful acquaintances who took pity on our motherless plight. The ladies of the United Methodist Women nominated my dad for the Mother of the Year. It's also possible that the house was owned by

Superior Steel. They operated the welding shop across the street and the red brick controls division next door. Dad and his brothers all had their first jobs on Barnett Road, sweeping slag off the floor of that shop.

Another rumor was that the house was burned as a training exercise for the Forest Park Fire Department. When I was in high school, I witnessed a burn exercise. It was a little yellow stucco house behind ours, vacant as long as I could remember. The scene was notable for its lack of urgency and surplus of equipment. Blocky firemen in full regalia tugged hoses into position while a handful of spectators unfolded lawn chairs. Finally, white smoke rippled under the eaves and the show began. The smoke increased and blackened. It formed a cloud the same volume as the house, a levitating double. Then we could see the red-orange glow of real fire inside, breathing and malevolent. The burning house pushed a wall of heat towards the crowd. Everyone dragged their lawn chairs back a few yards. The firemen pantomimed and aimed solid jets of water along the side of the house. The next afternoon, a bulldozer scraped up the blackened bits.

Not all houses will work for a burn exercise. The structure must be stripped of asbestos, lead, and glass, and be located a certain distance from inhabited residences and power lines. It must be forfeited, devalued, and futureless. There is virtually no tax advantage to burning your house down, but it's cheaper than demolition.

I could call the Fire Marshal's office and ask if they remember setting fire to my house. Or comb through the deed books at City Hall. I could find the owner of the Town & Country Mobile Home Park, one of two enduring fixtures on Barnett Road. It turns out his name is Burns and he's been there since 1983. I could find Albert, the other holdout. His junky shop is still there, hidden behind a rampart of rusted equipment.

I could ask anyone but Dad. We left Barnett Road when my father remarried in 1984. We moved into Gayle's house and changed schools. Our family of three became four, and then five when my brother was

born. It seemed nosy and mean to bring up the bad times that came
before.

Now all the houses on Barnett Road are gone, replaced by a warehouse complex called Air Logistics Center II. Next to the water tower
is clustered a two hundred foot telecom tower and a compact power
plant. On the other side of the street there's a long series of windowless warehouses instead of houses. This is one of many global locations of Hexion Chemical—a plastics manufacturer formed by the
merger of Eastman Chemical, Borden Chemical, and Bakelite. My old
block is now noted for "pollution, leaking underground tanks, chemical spills, and hazardous contamination sites." This data is provided
online for families with the privilege of researching neighborhoods
before they relocate—people who shop around for the good schools,
low crime, and distance from documented polluters. This information is not as relevant when you already live there, when someone
gives you a free place to stay, when you have nowhere else to go.

When we lived on Barnett Road, it was already transitioning to
an industrial zone. To the north was the vast State Farmers Market
with 150 acres of concrete docks, where tractor trailer trucks parked
with watermelons in June, pumpkins in September, and Frasier Firs
shortly after. To the west and south, Interstate 75 carved a wide river
of dead space. To the east, Barnett Road crossed Old Dixie Highway
and changed names, signaling the boundary of Rosetown, the black
neighborhood of Forest Park, as forbidding and sealed off to me as if
it were a gated community.

Above all, Barnett Road had the misfortune to be located one mile
from the Atlanta airport at the worst possible time. September 1980
marked the grand opening of the new Atlanta terminal, the largest
passenger complex in the world. Flight volume doubled overnight
and with it, the demand for runway expansion. When the airport
grows, everything it touches hardens into parking lots and warehouses. Above us, at all hours, hung a ceaseless strand of aircraft and
the grey drone of their engines. This was supposed to be a temporary

home for us; a brief interlude on the way to a more stable home. It was the last place my father expected me to make memories. But I still managed to get attached.

The child mind records the angle of light. We walked down to the dead end of Barnett Road, into the orange and spreading sun. Myra held one of Dad's hands, I held the other. We climbed the railroad tracks, Dad reminded us to look both ways. We balanced on the tracks behind the long, blank backside of a warehouse.

Dad clapped his hands and an echo bounced back, making us cheer.

"Hey!" shouted my sister.

A voice rebounded, "Hey."

Then it was my turn. "Hey, hey!" I piped. My echo replied, a warped soprano.

This went on many nights of the week. He let us take turns shouting until we'd had enough. Our shadows stretched all the way down the road.

The house on Phillips Drive, from a real estate flyer, 1997.

TEN

SLAGLE RESIDENCE

Just because I hated the house at 5026 Phillips Drive, doesn't mean I wanted it gone. First of all, the house belonged to Gayle. She cross-stitched and framed a little sign that said, GAYLE HARDEMAN, HOMEOWNER, 8-13-82, above an embroidered likeness of the house. It hung in the wood-paneled hallway with the family photos and *Gone With The Wind* commemorative plates. It was a fine starter house for a single girl, a fine place to visit while she and Dad were dating, but it was too small for the rest of us.

It looked like a child's drawing of a house—a short white rectangle with two shaded windows for eyes, a door for a nose, and a smiling curve of concrete that led from the front door to the driveway. Gayle chose the navy blue wallpaper pattern in the kitchen and the white wicker wastebasket in the bathroom. And yet our whole family lived there, crammed together, for thirteen years. Dad and Gayle had one bedroom and one closet, Myra and I shared the other, and then—surprise—our new baby brother arrived, so we converted the tiny porch into Lowell's bedroom. This one-thousand-square-foot box, bursting with stuff and noise, contained our family of five and a Scottish terrier who was never completely housebroken. We were supposed to answer the phone—a heavy beige touchtone with a curly cord—with a polite, "Slagle residence."

All the "Sargent Homes" were about the same size. Named for developer John Sargent, these tract cottages sprung up in rows around the Atlanta Army Depot when it opened in 1941. The houses were solid and precise. Each had matching hardwood floors, respectable oak doors with crystal doorknobs, tiny basket-weave ceramic tiles on the bathroom floor and linoleum in the kitchen. Uniform concrete stairs led to each kitchen door, which was painted to coordinate with the trim on the scalloped awnings. Most of the houses on our block had identical floor plans, so a visit to the elderly lady next door produced the dim sensation of a parallel reality. It would have been a sensible house for a soldier returning from World War II, plus his bride. Both Dad's and Gayle's fathers were part of that wave of vets returning from the war and seeking blue collar jobs on the southside of Atlanta. They swelled the county population by 300 percent by 1960. Their kids and grandkids tripled this increase by 1990.

These houses were built for a time when people were thin and spry and lived modestly. The living proof of postwar prosperity, we were constantly fighting for space in that house. We squeezed past the piles of laundry in the photo-cluttered hallway. The washer and dryer served as kitchen counters when they weren't covered with books, mail, and groceries. On one end of the dining room table sat Gayle's sewing machine and an ever-present pile of pants to be hemmed and formal dresses to be altered. On the other end, Dad cleared off a square foot of table to prepare his Sunday school lessons. A thick paperback Bible and coffee cup were his early morning companions. We all found ways to carve out our space.

By the early '90s, most Sargent Homes had been customized beyond recognition with pastel painted exteriors, awnings removed, or decks appended. Residents expanded their living space with a low budget addition on the back or a bigger porch out front. These modifications were never quite seamless. You couldn't buy that asbestos siding anymore.

Forest Park also expanded as a bedroom community of the young Atlanta Municipal Airport. In 1961 it was the region's first jetport.

In 1981, with the opening of the modern terminal, the newly named
Hartsfield International Airport became the biggest, busiest, and
noisiest in the world. When I was a kid, 700,000 flights a year connected through Hartsfield, and most of them brushed over the back
yards and football fields of Forest Park.

By 1989, the FAA's noise mitigation program finally reached
our neighborhood on Phillips Drive. Friends at church and school
talked about getting new windows, doors, and insulation installed
in exchange for their "air rights." The airport offered a combo deal
whereby residents who participated in their "acoustical treatment
program" were automatically required to sign over an "avigation
easement" for their property. Though no one ever used the legal term,
these easements restricted the property owner's right to interfere with
avigation, or aerial navigation, by planting trees, building towers or
installing lighting. At the same time, they protected the airport against
liability for impacts of noise, pollution, vibration, or other nuisances
of living in the flight path. Our house was slightly south of the noisiest
districts and not eligible for the program. Nevertheless, the oppres-
sive roar of descending jets interrupted phone calls and TV viewing
at our house.

I tolerated the airplanes, but savored the clatter of trains at night.
I lay in bed listening to the retreating steam whistle and fantasized
about hopping a boxcar.

We had no air conditioning. Box fans in the windows hummed
along with the sound of crickets and trains. My sister and I had small
pink fans clamped to the ends of our beds, which on summer nights,
seemed to blow just enough hot air to dry our sweat. When I was in
high school, Myra and I got an AC window unit for our bedroom.
It smelled like a dank cellar and froze up predictably around 3:00
AM every morning. Either way, we fell asleep on top of our sheets,
dreamed of smothering, and woke up annoyed. More than once, I
curled up on the cool tile of the bathroom floor with the dog.

Our house was embarrassingly small, but I never felt poor. I
assumed the tiny house was a budgetary tradeoff. It meant that Gayle

could shop for name-brand groceries and big ticket Christmas presents. She wrote checks for Girl Scout camp, football camp, ballet, gymnastics, and guitar lessons. There was no cap on Easter dresses, back-to-school jeans, or all those uniforms and costumes. All three of us had bikes, braces, and birthday parties. Other than brief lessons on tithing, money was not much discussed in our house. We grew up with little concept of money, but no sense of deprivation. Gayle's homemade biscuits and cornbread made me feel at least as rich as the kids in bigger houses.

At the same time, I knew we weren't rich. On TV sitcoms, rich people had an upstairs and downstairs, they had swimming pools, wall-to-wall carpet, and multiple bathrooms. We all took turns with one tiny bathroom. First one up in the morning got to smell Dad's Old Spice aftershave lingering in the sink. Last one to bed at night could take a long, uninterrupted bath. There was no shower. I hated that there was no shower.

I was oblivious to the work that went into our home. My father and stepmother were constantly working on the house, maintaining it in ways I failed to notice. These changes happened on the weekends when I was visiting Mom. We came home on Sunday night and a change of furniture or coating of paint appeared from nowhere. I completely missed the conversion of the porch. The switch from our childhood bunk beds to simple twin beds happened while I wasn't paying attention. The grass got mowed, the bathtub scrubbed.

"Did you use something special to get it so white?" I asked Gayle, appraising her handiwork.

"Yeah," she said, laughing, "elbow grease."

I pretended to get the joke, afraid that she might assign the chore to me. Thus, I cultivated a willful incuriosity about the house. Like I shouldn't get too involved.

I hated that there was no privacy inside or out. Our house was at the end of Phillips Drive, where it met Forest Parkway and the train tracks. Less than a mile down the road was Jones Memorial United

Methodist Church, the setting of Dad and Gayle's wedding and the center of our social lives. Next door to the church was Lake City Elementary, where I transferred into the second grade. Farther up the hill was my middle school and high school. Each had a Phillips Drive address. Dad walked us home from school and pointed out the houses of people from church where we should knock if we ever got in trouble. He instructed my sister to walk on the side closest to the street, since she was older.

The whole town drove down Phillips Drive, so everyone saw us walking this way to and from school. One afternoon, Myra and I got into a fight as we walked. By the time we got home we had already forgotten the altercation, but Gayle was waiting for us with her hands on her hips. She had received a phone call from a concerned neighbor who reported that we were hitting each other over the head with our lunch boxes. Myra and I were astonished. How did she know? That was the hardest thing about our fights—trying to keep them quiet. We learned to cuss each other out in sign language, pinch each other in the back seat of the car, out of range of the rearview mirror, learned to jab and scratch each other in places that would be hidden by clothes. As soon as we got caught fighting, we were in trouble.

And when weren't we in trouble? We classic "children of divorce," sulking, bickering, perpetually on restriction. I honestly can't say if I was a bad or good child, but it seemed as if I was constantly in trouble. My sister and I were in trouble for being irresponsible and impolite, for disobeying the rules, half-assing our chores, smart-alecking our elders, and otherwise setting a poor example for our little brother. I got in trouble for skipping class and lying about it. Punishment was writing scripture a hundred times while sitting alone at the dining room table. Or it was sitting there with a plate of food and you couldn't get up until it was finished. It was washing the dinner dishes while the rest of the family watched TV, laughing loudly in the next room. Punishment was spankings, restriction, weeding the flower beds. But by a certain age, these strategies were exhausted and our punishment consisted

of interminable family conferences. We stood or sat for hours waiting for the verdict and the sentence. During these hours I faithfully
memorized the woodgrain in the table and the repeating pattern of the
wallpaper. My limbs fell asleep. Myra chewed her nails. The caning
of the dining room chairs imprinted on the back sides of our thighs.

We lived near the intersection with Forest Parkway, the four-lane
commercial thoroughfare crossing Forest Park from Fort Gillem to
the airport. When the house across the street from us went up for
sale, a commercial developer proposed to build a gas station and con-
venience store on the site. This required shifting the address from
Phillips Drive to Forest Parkway and rezoning the corner from residential to commercial.

This had to be my first lesson in land use. I remember going to City
Hall for the public hearing and watching my father stand up and testify that the twenty-four hour floodlights and additional traffic would
be devastating to our neighborhood. He looked small at the podium,
with his index cards in his back pocket. He articulated his argument
with the same firm intelligence and charm he used with his Sunday
school class. No matter. They tore down Mrs. Smith's house while I
was at school one morning. A dark brick bungalow that predated all
our cookie-cutter houses, it had an arched doorway and high peaked
roof. It was one of the nicest old houses on Phillips Drive.

"We lost, didn't we?" I said. "Why didn't they listen to you?"

Dad answered, "Money."

He said it like it was something filthy. It took me decades to process this comment. On the tax rolls for Clayton County, a house like
ours would be appraised at around $50,000. As a CVS Pharmacy, the
property would be worth $1.3 million. The Texaco station parcel was
recently valued at $724,000. In a struggling county, there was a real
economic incentive to flip our corner from residential to commercial
zoning.

My parents must have been sick about it. If Mrs. Smith's house
was a teardown, what was worth saving? I never heard them complain

about property values. The yellow construction equipment that leveled the hillside fascinated Myra, Lowell, and me. Once the workers went home, we climbed up on the bulldozer tread and traced its robot tracks through the firm red clay.

The new Texaco was immaculate. The soaring logo welcomed travelers from Forest Parkway. I marveled at the perfect concrete with freshly marked parking spaces. The air-conditioned rows of candy and wall-to-wall refrigerators of Coke. I snuck over before school in the mornings to buy Sour Punch Straws and Airheads.

The novelty wore off after a few months and we became the family that lived across the street from the Texaco. As a high schooler, I took advantage of the awkward situation. I instructed friends and dates to park at the Texaco—it was easier than trying to back out of our driveway onto Phillips Drive. Our tidy house with its red trimmed awnings and geranium beds was bathed in blue fluorescence all night long. We lived with that Texaco, which later became a glowing yellow Shell, for five or six years. Ultimately, it was another thing I hated about the house.

Around this time, my little brother went away for a week. Maybe the church youth group took a mission trip to Panama City Beach. Whatever the occasion, I prepared to greet him with a homemade "welcome home" poster. On a square of corrugated cardboard, under the headline, "THERE'S NO PLACE LIKE…" I drew a portrait of our house in scented Mr. Sketch markers. This rare display of nostalgia still sits on Lowell's desk. The cartoon house is sketched in licorice, adorned with mint-scented shrubs and cherry awnings. A citrus sun is breaking through the blue mango clouds. I spent years dreaming of escape, but the house became part of me, and such a big part that I couldn't continue hating it.

My parents managed to sell the house right after I left for college. All their preparations for the sale, the appraisals, the new roof, the potential buyers and offers—it all seems distant in my memory. The realtor's lockbox hung on the front door for months, maybe years.

What good parents they were to shield me from the grief and uncertainty of real estate. They finally joined with two adjacent neighbors and accepted an offer from a developer. Our property was summarily rezoned as commercial, with a permit to construct a CVS Pharmacy. I imagined the scene was like Mrs. Smith's house and the virgin Texaco—the bulldozers, dumpsters, and concrete trucks.

I learned of these developments by phone in my freshman dorm room. My parents were now, ironically, in a position to buy a lovely three-bedroom, two-and-a-half-bath ranch house on a large wooded lot in Jonesboro, about as far south of the airport as you can get and still be in Clayton County. They packed everything and moved without my help. Cool, I thought, they're finally getting out of there. Then the little house itself was moved—hoisted whole onto a flatbed truck and carted away. Where did it go? Were Dad and Gayle there to witness the spectacle? Looking back, I am shocked at my disconnection from this whole process. I see in this nonchalance a teenager's strident disdain for the past, a barely concealed desire to get the hell out of Forest Park forever.

While I was away at school, our Scottie dog vanished. He got lost, I guess, in the woods nearby and either found a new home or perished there. I kept up with the search by phone, thinking that as long as I wasn't there to note his absence, he wasn't really gone. I felt the same way about our old house.

I avoided Phillips Drive for a long time. One day I drove by and there was this large stucco confection where our house used to be, surrounded by oily blacktop and a ten-foot privacy fence. The new curbs and landscaping successfully removed any trace of our old driveway. I was tempted to stop and prowl the now unfamiliar grounds, but it was just another CVS, utterly anonymous. It was as though our house never existed, yet it became even heavier, more defined.

While my earliest childhood homes are vague and mythical, the house on Phillips Drive was memorized from years of wear and tear. I lived there from age six to seventeen, by far the longest I have ever lived anywhere. I knew the cracks in the driveway, the nandina bushes hugging the trashcans. I can picture the pixelated view of the back-yard through the screen of my bedroom window—Gayle's bug zapper glowing blue in the night. The secret soil under the spigot, shaded by elephant ears, behind the red-painted stoop where Dad hid his ashtray. That house was so small, you could lie in bed with your eyes closed and hear every movement of the family. Each particular set of bare feet on the hardwood floor, of cabinets opening and closing above the sink, the television murmuring whatever late night show I wasn't allowed to watch. When I dream of shuffling down a hallway, it's always that hallway. Or I'm driving down a hill and it's always Phillips Drive. I'm sailing into the driveway of 5026, right before the railroad tracks.

These are the default rooms of my random night wanderings. It is the home I drift to in all my weakness and spite.

Overgrown "noise land" in College Park.

ELEVEN

COUNTY RECORDS

I want to know who owns a piece of property.
How can I find out that information?

So begins the Frequently Asked Questions section of the Clayton County Tax Assessor's website. Real estate investors, developers, curious neighbors, and amateur detectives like myself are directed to the county records room, open to the public Monday through Friday.

I put off this visit for weeks, imagining the records room to be something like a legal library with hushed rows of elaborately coded file cabinets lined up under fluorescent light. Law clerks and real estate professionals moving expertly among shelves and computer stations. The thought of wandering these basement corridors to find information about my family seemed like the most hopeless kind of procrastination when I should really be interviewing my parents with these questions: How old was the house? What did it look like? Who owned it? When did we live there? When did we move? What happened to my house?

Then again, I had asked them everything, over dinner tables and coffee tables, and their memories were too vague. They tossed out scraps of memory. I resisted the urge to take notes. In all our conversations, I tried to remain nonchalant, and they responded with shrugs and meandering stories about the neighbors.

"Don't you remember, our neighbor's name was Stone? I always thought that was his first name, but maybe not. Ask your Dad, he remembers." Mom was always chatty about 133 South West Street.

"I bought it from an old lady, I think she was going into a nursing home," said Gayle, when asked about the house on Phillips Drive.

"I cleaned it out and my friends let me live there for free," said Dad, and that's all I know about Barnett Road.

I got the impression the details were jettisoned over the years as heavy, useless things. My baby was on the way. So I needed to go to the courthouse.

Highway 54, or Jonesboro Road, is the main north/south lifeline joining almost all the cities in a long, key-shaped county. It emerges from the southside of Atlanta and follows the railroad tracks through Forest Park, Lake City, Morrow, and Jonesboro, the county seat, and then continues south to Fayetteville's town square. In personal terms, it connects the Chick-fil-A where all my high school friends worked, Fort Gillem—a teeming and mysterious army depot—the Walmart, Waffle House, Southlake Mall, Tara Stadium, and Jason's brother's house, where he was living when we first started dating. I got a driver's license so I could drive to see him.

When my parents were teenagers, Jonesboro Road included long stretches of scrub pine forest and leftover farmland between towns. But in my memory, it has always been one long ugly strip of congestion and bad signage, where one small city melted into the next.

In the driving sprawl of Atlanta, the quality and design of roadside signage are your first indicator of an area's affluence. Planned cities like Fayetteville and Peachtree City have ordinances that restrict the height and scale of roadside signs, so even a typical McDonalds is marked with a tastefully landscaped "M." As I drove south to visit the county courthouse, the traffic wasn't bad, but the signs were worse than ever. Jonesboro Road is a free-market riot of cheap, backlit, litter-on-a-stick ads, all competing to be the biggest and ugliest, with no apparent regulation. There were signs within signs: Harold's

BBQ, a southside institution, has a bold blue "bank-owned" sign out front. The name of Connor's Florist, another local independent, was white-washed over. Even the big chains had withered and retreated. An old McDonalds, Waffle House, and Hardee's, stripped of their logos, were still easy to identify. The sign in front of Hardee's said "Specials."

To be fair to Clayton County, my sour view of this scene on an otherwise calm and blue September morning was likely caused by my own dawning apprehension more than the blight itself. I had to reckon with my own unbalance as I sat in the parking lot of the charming 1880s courthouse waiting for my anxiety and morning sickness to subside. I walked towards the old courthouse, with its brick red towers and peaks, its four-faced clock looming overhead. I hadn't been to this place since that frazzled and sweltering summer day eight years earlier when Jason and I applied for a marriage license.

I followed signs to the tax assessor's office, through the double doors, up a single flight of stairs, where the smell of new carpet and paint caused me to stall on the landing, dizzy and winded. As I approached the receptionist's desk, I had that self-consciousness familiar at hospital admissions desks and airline ticket counters—the sense of misplaced and inexpressible urgency before a uniformed government functionary whose chief priority is to keep people like me in line.

"I'd like to look at some old tax maps," I started.

I had already messed up. The middle-aged black woman behind the desk cocked an eyebrow. "Old maps?" she said and began shaking her head.

"Because the properties don't exist anymore," I continued. "They won't appear on the current maps."

"Well, if they don't exist," she trailed off. "Do you know the address?"

"Yes!"

"Then you can start on the wall map. You know our system? The big numbers are the district, the little grey numbers are the land lot."

I stepped over to a map that covered the wall opposite her desk.
The room was quiet, cushioned. I could hear two ladies in conversation in the neighboring office. "Well, what's he locked up for? Shoot."

I was grateful for the low, carpeted box at the foot of the map. I
stood on it and my toes to look at the northernmost corner of the
county. I was grateful that no one else was there, waiting for me to fin-
ish, waiting for their turn with the map, because the tiny street names
were making me woozy and I worried that my pounding heart would
give me away as a fraud and a terrorist, not just an innocent citizen
looking into public records.

"You got it?" asked the lady.

"I got the district. The little grey numbers..."

"They're green," she said. I still couldn't tell if she was trying to
be helpful.

The map began to make sense. I busied myself with note taking.
South West Street was in the 13th District, land lot 12. The house
on Phillips Drive was also the 13th, land lot 49. And Barnett Road
was right next to that, 13-52. It was marked "Industrial Area." Seeing
these places formalized into a numbered system gave me some hope.
Maybe it's not all random, I thought; maybe there is some planning,
some purpose.

THE ENTIRE COUNTY WAS CONTAINED in about sixty large books of
maps, arranged in custom racks along the wall. As I maneuvered the
13th District book out of its slot and onto the counter, the front desk
lady approached me.

"Ma'am?" she called out. There was no one else in the room.

"Ma'am. It's time for my fifteen minute break." She was tying the
laces of her bright white athletic shoes. "So if you need any help, just
ask those ladies in the next room. And if you need copies, they're five
dollars apiece. Cash or check."

I thanked her and turned back to the map. We were alone.

The huge plat book, bound with faux black leather, clamped a couple hundred yellowed maps between a marvelous expanse of gold and burgundy and turquoise marbled end pages. I needed both hands to spread the three-foot pages open. I turned them carefully, even though there was no one to judge my respectful technique. Each land lot was further divided into sub plats, each plat was followed by a series of lined pages where the names of the owners were recorded in pencil.

5026 Phillips Drive was the easiest to find, as it was the most recently demolished, or "voided," and I actually knew the name of the owner. I found Gayle's maiden name etched in a cell of the vast page on 8/13/82, right between Blanch Gentry (7/26/77) and Realmark Equities Corp (1/28/97). I recognized the names of our neighbors: Taylor, Fannie J. and Abney, Glen Alvin, all scrawled in someone's teacherly cursive. They all had identical sales dates to Realmark Equities Corp and the map showed they were combined and voided in 1998. The new property changed owners once again and became CVS Retail Store #165 on 5/6/98. God, they were tiny lots, just sixty feet across the front and a hundred feet deep. So many little houses were crammed on the page, at least a hundred, like the lines of a parking lot.

Barnett Road was just a few pages away, but the map was a puzzle. There was no sign of the residential plots where my house might have been, just large industrial lots marked Atlanta Air Logistics and Georgia Power Co. I flipped to the ledger and began reading the list of names from the bottom up. I was looking for names I might recognize, a game I often played when walking my dog in the cemetery by our house. The family names of my classmates and teachers and church friends and doctors appear in the rows of graves—Bartlett, Boyd, Phillips, Stone, Mahoney. I know the names, the names are part of the landscape.

I scanned upwards through the list of strangers and corporations and finally hit the top, the names I was looking for—Harold Benefield and Wendell Kitchens, 7/1/81—two of my father's best friends. They bought the property just before we moved in. They bought it from the

Barnettes and the Benefields, older couples I remembered from my grandparents' Sunday school class. Suddenly I am reconstructing the story...Harold and Wendell bought the property as an investment, and the timing was perfect to help out my Dad. The favor cemented my Dad's loyalty for life, but the house was never considered a serious option as a residence. By 1984, they had sold the land and adjoining parcels to Georgia Power Co. I love Harold and Wendell now. I love their little names in pencil in the book. But I was going to need an older map that actually showed where the house used to be.

"Excuse me, ma'am?" I timidly interrupted a lady playing solitaire on her computer. "Is it possible to look at older versions of these maps?"

"You don't want those. They aren't current," she said and quickly led me away from her desk.

I explained my dilemma and she gave me directions to the Courthouse Annex across the street where all the old maps were kept. Why was everyone so quick to tell me no?

On my short walk I observed no citizens, no customers, no business being done. Only a couple of orange-vested landscapers discussing the stipulations of their parole. Of the three police officers operating the small metal detector entrance to the annex, two were filling out crossword puzzles. At the tax commissioner's office I saw four women casually gathered around a desk chatting, with no customers, no phone calls, nothing to do but wait for their fifteen-minute break. I stewed over the time I was taking off work to be here, the emails and voicemails piling up on my desk, and compared it to the pace of this sleepy small town workday.

I was met with more courteous "No's." The record room was closed, they said. Or it was under construction. Well, I guess you can look around in there, but it's dusty and dirty.

I dug into the piles of maps, marked by decade and coated with a layer of unnaturally white dust. The 1981 book showed our precise lot on Barnett Road and the old house in Mountain View. Tammie Joe Davis sold it to the City of Atlanta on 9/30/81.

Then it was No, you can't make copies. Well, let me ask. No, you'll
have to file an Open Records Request with the Commissioner. It'll
take two weeks and they're five dollars a copy. Is he in his office? No.
He's in a meeting. No, you can't take photos of the pages.

I think even they got tired of telling me no, or I turned on my
sweetest Clayton County accent, because I left the office grinning and
thanking them with copies of three maps under my arm. I had entered
with the beginnings of an anxiety attack, cursing this lousy, slack-ass
county, but I left practically skipping. I had documented evidence of
all three of my lost houses.

On the drive back north, I decided to avoid the tacky main thoroughfare and follow the two-lane along the other side of the railroad
tracks. I passed the "Road to Tara" Museum in the old Jonesboro
train depot, across from the Cemetery of Confederate Dead with its
rebel flag flying high, and was startled to arrive a few blocks later at
Highway 138 at the site of my parents' wedding in 1974.

The tree was gone, but I knew that was the corner. It used to be an
extension of the courthouse, but now it's the C. Crandle Bray Police
Headquarters Building. There used to be a tremendous old oak tree
on that corner, one of those with branches that extend to form a furry
green globe. Once I drove by it with my mom and she said, "Oh
honey! Your father and I got married under that tree!" Just like that.

I had never seen wedding photos or heard anything about a tree.
Yet Mom and Dad often tossed out these comments like I knew what
they were talking about. My complete knowledge of their life and
times together consisted of such offhand remarks and the fictions
they inspired. Were they barefoot with flowers in their hair? Did they
sweet-talk a justice of the peace into stepping outside to perform the
ceremony? Jason and I were able to get away with such things; it's a
wonder what rules people will break for a charming young couple.

IT HADN'T RAINED ALL month, but the convicts were out in orange
vests mowing the dirt. Three zero-turn mowers whipped crazily

around the shallow lawn in front of the Harold R. Banke Justice Center, churning up a dust cloud that floated out over Tara Boulevard. This was the new county courthouse, the real one, a bustling, modern complex designed on the big box model—a vast parking lot encircling the slab-like brick structure.

It looms up glassy and new from the scrubland on Tara Boulevard at the edge of the county line. Highway 19/41 travels the full length of Clayton County, from Mountain View to this vaguely rural point in Jonesboro, ten miles south. This is the same Highway 41 that connects Chicago to Miami. Through Clayton County, we call it Old Dixie Highway and Tara Boulevard. The roadway is crusted with pawn shops, payday lenders, Western Union posts, and discount malls, all housed in former gas stations and fast food joints that bear the shape of their original function. The cheap signs for Royal Spa and TitleBucks Pawn decorated the strip in primary colors—red, yellow, green, and blue. It occurred to me that maybe they're not tearing down buildings fast enough around here.

As I drove south against morning rush hour, I dismantled one rice cake after another and let the salty grains dissolve in my mouth. Rice cakes and green apples were practically the only foods I could tolerate, and I needed a supply every few hours to fend off the nausea. My doctor pointed out that this menu contained almost no calories or nutrition. I was losing weight. Tiny rice crumbs fell across my lap like dandruff.

Gradually the strip trailed off and the highway narrowed to four lanes. At the undeveloped frontier of Clayton County stood the new Justice Center. I squinted up at the massive façade, with its looming stucco columns and flags whipping in the blue air. A plane crossed the sky incredibly slowly, the size and shape of a minnow.

I remember when this courthouse was under construction. It was the summer Jason graduated from college and was living with his brother in a nearby subdivision. I was crashing with Dad and Gayle for the summer, in their house that I was stubborn about not calling "home." And so we found ourselves together in Jonesboro, back in the suburbs with no place to go. All summer, we ventured down unmarked dirt roads looking for places to have sex. What we found were construction sites. Whole gated neighborhoods of half-built homes that belonged to the crickets at night. I loved the cool concrete and the clean smell of pine framing timbers. The corners were scattered with construction workers' cigarette butts, Gatorade bottles, and Doritos wrappers. They didn't seem like real places yet.

The entire county was under construction. By now, families have grown up in those houses. The owners in those fresh, new houses never dreamed that we were there first, deciphering the master bed-room from the skeletal layout.

We only got caught once, and it was at the Justice Center construc-tion site. A police car aimed its high beams on us as we were staking out a location—fully dressed—in the moonlight. I hadn't been back there since.

A plaque in the lobby said the building was dedicated on November 3, 2000. That means we were prowling the grounds in the summer of 1999. The institutional architecture was meant to fill me with awe. Instead, I had to smirk. I had seen this building naked.

Here, the security guards were actually working. Court was in ses-sion throughout the building. Men in suspenders and suits finished their cell phone conversations in English and Spanish before passing through the metal detector. Their clipped words bounced around the glass and marble foyer.

I found my way downstairs to the Deeds and Land Records office. Here was the room I had imagined—a beige vault with row after row of numbered books. A dozen legal professionals moved purposefully through the racks—title examiners, I later learned. I flinched each time they slammed the heavy volumes onto the counter and began flipping unceremoniously through the pages. I crept over to the index books and gingerly slid one off the shelf. More crashes echoed from the racks.

This wasn't a library. This room contained a record of every property transaction in the county's young 150-year history. Each family drama, divorce, death, inheritance, and foreclosure, was coded into a document, notarized, and filed here for posterity. Are these the only copies? I wondered. The prospect evoked the irresistible image of the fire that might pour through this room, lighting up the books for a moment before they tumbled into ash.

Starting with the oldest known property owner (or "grantee"), I traced the ownership of all three of my houses back as far as I could. All three jumped from commercial developers back through a series of homeowners to the individual landowners at the turn of the century. 133 South West Street went from Highwoods Realty back to E.R. Stewart in 1901. 5026 Phillips Drive went from Retail Ventures Group Inc. to Henry A. Phillips in 1897. And 110 Barnett Road leapt from Atlanta Air Logistics Center, LLC. back to Mrs. Martha L. Porter in 1908. So many names and deeds, but the pattern was simple: in each case, large rural tracts were developed into residential subdivisions. As the neighborhoods expired, the lots were consolidated back into industrial zones. A time-lapse map image would show the land processed from forest to farmland to houses to concrete. The whole cycle took less than a century.

As the hours passed, I became better acquainted with the massive deed books. It was not a complicated process. I pulled them from their neatly numbered racks and mashed them flat on the glass face of a copier. I highlighted names and years on the photocopies. I marveled at strange little discoveries—Juanita Rogers died in 1976 and her daughter inherited the house on Phillips Drive. Here was the explanation of the ghost Mama Gayle claimed to have seen in the hallway. And there was the constant spark of recognition as I spotted names that I knew from the corner street signs of my neighborhood. Ewing Street, Bartlett Road, and Phillips Drive were in fact, men—Albert, John, and Henry.

After a while, the ladies behind the reception desk went to lunch. I buried my nausea in the deeds. I was so close, I thought, to real evidence of my houses. Some descriptions popped up in long strings of legalese and then disappeared in the next transaction—"this being improved property with a house and garage apartment thereon" or "this being improved property and having a one-story frame house thereon." A house was only notable as an "improvement"—which is code for an increase in tax value. And the value of the property was always hidden in legal terms like "ten dollars and other valuable consideration," and in a much older deed, "one dollar and love and affection." These terms were a substitute for a public record of the transaction. So what good were the public records? There was no mention of when the houses were built, or who built them, how grand or humble they might have been. No record of their demolition or departure. The address never appears in the deed. You can trace the history of a property; it's much harder to trace a house.

I slowly registered that the only way to find out the real story about a house is to question the former owners. Owners who, I imagined, were aging or dead, with failing memories or the desire to forget. "Take care in infringing on the personal lives of previous owners or relatives," warned the authors of a Smithsonian article *How to Research the History of Your House*. "They may have painful memories which they do not wish to remember, or they may just not want to be bothered." When Jason and I started shopping for a house, our real estate agent warned us about accepting anecdotal evidence of a house's age or price. "Everyone lies about how much they paid," he told me. "Make sure to check the records."

What was I doing here? There were no records, only hearsay. I lay my forehead on a wooden lectern in a forest of 10,000 deed books. The houses seemed even more ephemeral than when I began. I don't even remember what color they were. I gathered my photocopies of deeds and maps into three little piles, one for each house, and left the record room.

I knew one of the names I highlighted on the deed for Barnett Road was alive and well and remembered my old house. In fact, he worked in this very courthouse. Chief Justice Harold G. Benefield, my father's best friend, could be upstairs in court right now. Maybe he would talk to me.

Outside, the wind had picked up and small clusters of leaves tumbled against the curb. I made the long hike across the parking lot, shielding my notes from the wind. I could hear the hollow whistle of distant airplanes and a bitter taste filled my throat. Unlike the old courthouse, this place would not be worth restoring in a hundred years.

Just before I reached the car, I started dry heaving. I moved quickly to a strip of grass and willed my stomach to stay still. A woman with a cell phone by her ear paused by her Honda, looking at me. Don't worry, I wanted to say, it's just morning sickness. I hadn't told anyone besides Jason that I was pregnant.

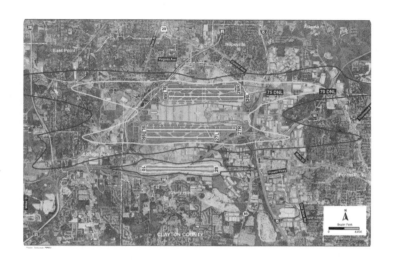

Airport Area Noise Contours, City of Atlanta Department of
Aviation, Draft Environmental Assessment, 2007.

TWELVE

OUR AIRPORT

My parents met us for dinner at a Thai restaurant in Hapeville that overlooked the airport. While there is no airport-sanctioned public observation deck, a few balconies along Virginia Avenue offer a glimpse of the swarming activity on the tarmac. Between mid-rise hotels, white planes with dark fins roll silently along a distant taxiway. Curious little vehicles swarm in the dust clouds left by landing aircraft.

As we waited for our meal, Dad leaned over to Gayle and asked, "What does that remind you of?" He pointed to a crumbly strip of concrete below.

She smiled. "Going to the airport."

Jason and I examined the mysterious strip and its twin across the street. They were about fifty yards long, unmarked, overgrown with weeds, and disconnected from any roadway. My parents have done this as long as I can remember—shared inside jokes and memories at the dinner table while we tried to guess what they're talking about.

Eventually Dad explained that we were looking down on the former entrance to the Atlanta Municipal Airport, the dramatic symmetrical ramps that led to the old terminal. I couldn't understand why the entrance and exit ramps remained. Why were they left behind? Everything disappears in Atlanta, why not those lackluster remnants?

The entire Atlanta Municipal Airport would fit in one parking lot of today's Hartsfield-Jackson International Airport. The whole thing was gone, but for some reason the entrance and exit ramps survived. Cut off and floating, they led nowhere and served no purpose. What planning oversight or sentimental urge allowed them to remain? The remaining concrete was like part of a secret map, visible only from the air.

I asked my dad if he was a frequent flyer in those days. He thought that was funny.

"We were always picking someone up or dropping them off. I didn't fly for the first time until I was in my forties."

Watching planes at the Atlanta Airport was a legitimate date activity for a whole generation of Atlantans. Then he told me about "Blue Lights," a notorious destination for teenage necking on the College Park end of the runways. The long stretches of pavement were marked by low blue runway lamps, and virtually unsupervised.

I did the math. As Forest Park natives, Dad and Gayle grew up with the airport, but it was the 1990s before they ever actually flew anywhere. By then, it was a completely different airport—new name, entrance, tower, and terminal. It had become a place equipped to handle four times the passenger volume, and that volume included the very residents it had displaced.

I was seated next to the window, uncomfortably warm as the sunset glare baked my cardigan, but I kept it on. The square of gauze taped in the crook of my elbow was left from a routine blood draw. My parents would notice it and ask about it and I still hadn't told them anything about being pregnant. I wasn't even admitting it to myself.

It had taken two years and two miscarriages to get this far along in a healthy pregnancy. When we started trying to get pregnant, I couldn't imagine the hormonal wilderness ahead. According to Facebook, it seemed like all my girlfriends had such a pleasant time having babies.

Meanwhile, miscarriage is death without ceremony. No funeral, no name. No one would ever tell you, for example, if your mother died, that mother-death is actually quite common, hang in there honey, you'll find another mother. The angst of miscarriage lingers, maybe even multiplies, because you're the only one who knew the deceased, and the way you knew them was theoretical, fleeting. You conjured them into existence, only you conjured poorly and it is probably your fault the spell failed.

The first thing people ask is, how far along were you? As if to measure the loss. A couple of months for me each time, but it was years of plotting, taking jobs, situating rooms and relationships, hours and dollars. Adding insult to injury are the relentless announcements and baby showers, the perils of visiting a Target at 10:00 AM on a weekday. Pregnant friends everywhere, as if generated by my own misfortune.

Two losses in a row put me in the mode of self-protective detachment. It wasn't until after the first trimester, after a high risk, high-res ultrasound at thirteen weeks showed not only "a keeper" but a healthy baby boy, that I began to consider that this was a potential family member I was ignoring. The doctor said, "Try to have fun. Try not to worry." But I was grim as I called my family to tell them the news, cutting off any celebration or questions. Even so, my mom sent me a blue teddy bear and flowers the next day.

Sorry kid, but your first few weeks of existence were a time of profound silence and dread. Instead of creating my baby registry, I was digging through county deed records, verifying rumors and stories about the airport. I carried you with me to all the ragged edges of the runways. You were acclimated to plane noise before you were born.

I HEARD SO MANY STORIES of villainous airport encroachment, even legitimate accounts began to sound like conspiracy theories.

I heard that the airport was built on top of the Flint River, or the headwaters of the river, which is Georgia's second longest and a major southeastern watershed. This turned out to be true. Though it resembles a drainage ditch where it meets the northern runways through a supersized pipe, by the time the Flint emerges on the south side of the world's busiest airport it looks like an urban creek winding through a forest. It's a place where the brave might dig for crawdads, though not yet deep enough to canoe.

The shallow bowl of the Flint River basin was the ideal terrain for a racetrack, which later became Candler Field, then Hartsfield-Jackson airport. Channelized and buried since at least the 1960s, the secret Flint River is both a marvel of engineering and a metaphor for the area's hidden soul. As the airport grew up around it, the ancient river continued silently on its way to the Gulf of Mexico.

I heard that the airport once tried and failed to convert Virginia Avenue, the main commercial strip north of the airport, where Thai Heaven is located, into a runway. This is false. Having steeped myself in airport master plans, I knew this didn't make sense, but I could understand the basis for rumor. From shifting Interstate 85 to erasing the entire City of Mountain View to building a runway on top of I-285, wilder things had happened during ATL's climb to aviation dominance.

For College Park residents, these were not rumors, but a genuine existential threat. The College Park Historical Society was formed by concerned residents in 1978 to fight northward expansion of the airport. That same year they would have been watching events in Mountain View unfold—the mayor on trial, scores of houses lined up on flatbed trucks, the scandal in the newspaper: "City Charter Revoked."

Over the next two decades, they succeeded in registering 850 houses and the Main Street commercial corridor on the National Register of Historic Places, creating one of the largest historic districts in the state and protecting the core of College Park from further threats. They successfully fought off proposals for flight vectors that would aim additional air traffic over their homes, plus round-the-clock cargo flights that would generate noise through the night.

In the same way, over the last decade I have found countless groups of Airport-area exiles who congregate on Facebook to post black-and-white class photos and front yard snapshots. Their posts are tiny acts of historic preservation, just trying to remind each other of what the neighborhoods looked like before they were absorbed by the airport.

Meanwhile, the airport continued to acquire vast swaths of College Park neighborhoods under the flight paths for purposes other than runways and aeronautical uses. These not-so-historic places met their ignoble ends as airport parking lots, a rental car center, and a gigantic convention center.

I heard one story that sounded so preposterous, I thought it must be a rumor. A friend from high school told me that a Chuck Norris movie was shot in College Park in the 1980s and the filmmakers blew up a whole neighborhood of airport-owned houses. This friend was working in the film industry and he heard the story firsthand, from a guy who participated in the production. That's the only reason I didn't dismiss it immediately as a paranoid urban legend.

It turned out to be true. *Invasion USA* was a 1985 low-budget action thriller filmed in several Atlanta locations, including a battle scene downtown involving tanks on Peachtree Street. According to online movie trivia, the Soviet terrorists in *Invasion USA* blew up several houses near the Atlanta Airport that had been slated for demolition due to runway expansion.

I found this neighborhood attack scene online and advanced slowly through the footage to look at the houses. It was an intersection that looked like any early 1960s neighborhood on the southside—modest brick ranch houses notched into a hill, surrounded by full and towering pines. They had picture windows with white shutters and long driveways and carports where station wagons and boats were parked. The scene was shot at night, presumably on Christmas Eve, and their eaves and holly bushes were loosely draped with strings of red and green bulbs.

The scene opened with an instrumental version of "Hark the Herald Angels Sing" as a pack of kids scampered from their bikes to their front doors for supper. The music shifted to a sinister synth soundtrack as a large pickup truck rolled into the frame. Two bad guys wearing goggles stood in the back, one blonde, one masked, passing a bazooka back and forth and taking aim at the houses.

The first blast jogged the camera. Blurry extras ran screaming as the house exploded. In slow motion, the fireball hurled an entire door, still attached to its jamb, across the yard. A ladder toppled away from a Christmas tree. The terrorist grinned, pivoted, and fired on more houses. It appeared that he detonated at least eight of them before patting the top of the pickup truck and signaling their work was done.

I couldn't bring myself to watch the rest of the movie, so I have no idea what led up to this perverse scene, or what happened afterwards. I assume it sets Norris up to unmercifully punish the bad guys. An attack on suburbia on Christmas Eve is an intentionally disturbing scene, but it made my stomach hurt for different reasons. While most airport homes were unceremoniously demolished, the near-pornographic destruction of this corner of College Park is stashed on YouTube for all to witness.

I can't believe this happened in 1984. I thought this kind of scorched-earth urban renewal ended in the 1960s.

The production crew didn't bother to change the street signs, so I was able to freeze on a frame that included a tiny "First Ave" sign and then locate First Avenue on a 1969 airport map. First Avenue was on the southwest side of the airport, near a subdivision called Newton Estates. I zoomed into an odd, triangular intersection that matched the footage. The airport's rental car center covers it now.

Searching for Newton Estates in the airport's environmental records led me to a remarkable document, The Hartsfield-Jackson Atlanta International Airport Noise Land Reuse Plan. It was an enormous and formal report, consisting of two hundred low-quality scans of legalese, maps and charts. It explained the FAA's methodology for measuring decibel levels near the airport as "day night average sound levels" or DNL. The worst affected areas were within these "noise contours." The runways were circled in red for greater than 75 DNL, the highest noise level. The yellow 70-75 DNL contour spilled out beyond the runways to the east and west into College Park and Clayton County. The green noise contour, 65-70 DNL was a blob that nearly swallowed the southside. Within these boundaries, the airport could apply for federal funds to buy out residences, churches, and other "incompatible uses" on designated "noise land." These were the lines that determined where people could live.

Most fascinating to me were the hundreds of spreadsheets detailing every single parcel acquired by the airport from the early 1980s through 2009, including the purchase price, date of transaction, and the source of federal funds used to make the purchase. I knew that every single line of data represented a family, a business owner, or a pastor seated across from a team of attorneys at a closing table. Each line on the spreadsheet marked a turning point.

My home in Mountain View was nowhere to be found in these records. It was part of a pilot program that preceded the airport's official noise mitigation efforts, early attempts to stem residential complaints about the racket. Also missing were the huge swaths of College Park, Riverdale, and other neighborhoods that are underneath the runways and terminals today. Only those useless parcels designated as "noise land" were documented in detail because the airport would eventually need to "dispose" of them and convert them into "compatible uses" like warehouses, parking lots, and light industrial uses.

I studied the document into the early hours of the morning, pondering the scale of the Hartsfield-Jackson's kingdom. How could this land acquisition program be so enormous, so obvious, and yet so misunderstood by the people who lived there? It was upsetting to think that the relocation of Mountain View was not an isolated undertaking, a thing of the past, but an ongoing, continuous campaign. The transactions seem to peak in the mid '80s, but airport buyouts continued through the next twenty years.

I found the First Avenue parcels used in *Invasion USA* in the airport's Noise Land inventory. Scrolling through the pages and pages of transactions is strange and unbearable, but I did it. I counted 571 residential transactions in this area alone. Closing dates clustered around 1984, 1985, and 1986, which means that during the production of the film, this area wasn't completely vacant. While the buyouts were still in progress, high-powered explosives were violently shaking the neighborhood. Invading, indeed.

Chuck Norris has a sufficient cult following to have merited a short documentary called *The Making of Invasion USA*. In it, the director, dead eyed in a pink Hawaiian shirt, boasts, "We did, in fact, really destroy the neighborhood."

There was some B-roll footage of the crew decorating the outside of houses with tinsel and lights in their final hours. The interior shots of pyrotechnicians rigging one house with mortars were even more poignant. Here were rooms from 1984 that matched a whole catalog of ghost houses from my childhood. A quick shot of patterned linoleum in the kitchen, a dark floor register in the carpet, candy pink tile in the bathroom. I watched this part in slow motion.

A MONTH LATER, ON A Friday night after work, Jason rode MARTA a few extra stops to meet me at the airport for a date. I waited by the entrance to the train station. The orange sodium lights and abrupt end of air conditioning signaled that you were leaving the airport, trading one mode of transportation for another, less comfortable one.

We were there because I wanted to see the photo exhibit commemorating the thirtieth anniversary of the new "midfield" terminal. It's an entirely different experience to visit the world's busiest airport when you aren't determined to catch a flight or locate an arriving traveler. It reminded me of going to a mall at Christmas—lots of people, very focused and hustling.

Instead of looking at the massive overhead "Arrivals and

Departures" board, you might observe the virtuosity of the piano man at Houlihan's Bar & Grille. Without hurrying towards your gate, you might notice the small tribe of homeless men taking advantage of the facilities. When you're not a captive audience, you might think twice about the price of candy. It's like $3.99 for a bag of Sour Patch Kids.

The "exhibit" consisted of a few photos and architectural renderings mounted to the pillars of the grand atrium. As we cruised around the columns, taking photos of photos, reading the captions aloud to each other and generally giggling and acting amused, a few busy commuters paused to assess the exhibit. It's hard to explain why we found it so entertaining.

Maybe because the airport has been such an enormous presence in our lives, and this was like a rare chance to view the family album. Mayor Maynard Jackson and his wife Valerie were there, cutting ribbons alongside a baby-faced Governor Jimmy Carter and the young Shirley Franklin, who would go on to become mayor. The CEOs of Delta and Eastern were posed in a moment of rare camaraderie.

At the anniversary ceremony, George Berry, who served as general manager during the transition, made a speech:

> That day had to be one of the high points of all our lives, every one of us who worked on it, dreamed about it, and who thought that being a part of such a dramatic undertaking would be something that would mark us for the rest of our lives—and it has.

I wrote down the date: September 21, 1980. This date must have marked my life too, and the lives of most southside residents, in ways that are hard to estimate. It meant the official end of many residential communities around the airport.

The exhibit did a good job of comparing the airport before and after this grand opening ceremony, making a case that the enormous new airport was inevitable. Both the 1961 and the 1980 terminals were the biggest, most advanced airports of their day, and both assured Atlanta's ranking as the busiest passenger airport in the world. The original airport, as described in *Air Castle of the Jet Age* was "all sparkling blue and white...spread out like a giant fiddler crab in that sea of asphalt and concrete."

Designing for maximum efficiency, terminal engineers took it as a compliment when Paul Goldberger, architecture critic for *The New York Times*, wrote, "it is hard not to get over the sense that one is caught in a huge machine, something like a great Xerox machine." Unlike the "jet age" generation of airports, which served as a hopeful, symbolic gateway to a city, this new terminal was designed to accommodate the high volume demands of transferring passengers and cargo.

A series of promotional photos showed the new terminal in all its vacant glory. Before, it was all glittering tile, potted plants, and "The Oasis Lounge." After, the Xerox machine welcomed travelers with acres of burgundy carpet, molded plastic chairs, and chrome. Lots of chrome.

I FOUND A JULY 1984 home movie of the original terminal demolition that someone posted online. The Super-8 footage gave everything a golden haze. The scene opened on blue sky with a buzzing sound, as if air traffic continued amidst the planned implosion. The new control tower was already in use and construction on the fourth runway was underway. The camera focused on the 1961 tower, rigged with explosives. It was a delicate puzzle box of alternating stripes—aqua windows and blue curtain wall—crowned with a glass turret. The building anchored a series of high-flying arched pavilions.

There was a wobbly 360-degree pan, as if the cameraman was just killing time before the countdown. The tops of people's heads. Block letters on the adjacent building spelled out FLY EASTERN AIRLINES. In the foreground, the crowd shifted. They stood by their cars. Then the news helicopters moved out of the frame.

Back to the tower. The faint chant of a countdown could be heard. At zero, the implosion began. It sounded exactly like the sound effect for thunder in a cartoon. As the crash subsided, the building slipped down evenly behind a rising wall of dust. It looked two-dimensional, like a plywood stage prop lowered behind a set. About four seconds is all it took.

Cheers. Applause.

"Aw man," a voice off camera said. "It just disappeared didn't it?"

Cut to a helicopter drifting through the dust cloud. Chatter and whoops from the crowd. A woman's nervous laughter. Pulverized concrete bloomed out toward the parking lot.

Cut to the dust cloud, now from a distance. Small figures moved to their cars.

JASON AND I PICKED OVER OUR Styrofoam plates of ten-dollar chow mein; I had recently learned that noodles were one of the few foods I could tolerate. As we watched people milling in the food court, I considered our date night at the airport a southside tradition. For generations we have come to these grounds for romance and adventure, either at anticipating a flight, parking at "Blue Lights," or watching the planes takeoff. That fuzz of hopeful pre-flight anxiety happens at the airport even when you're not traveling.

Maybe it was the weight of the pregnancy, but I was glad not to be going anywhere. It was calming to be a stone in in the river of travelers. I kept my eye on the homeless and runaways wandering these halls, just here for the scenery.

THIRTEEN

BARNETT ROAD

The corner of Barnett Road and Old Dixie Highway was flanked by a slick new Exxon gas station and the Town & Country Mobile Home Park. The morning sky was crossed with contrails and the scaffolding of a tall telecommunications tower. As I waited in my car, I imagined the dissipating jet exhaust, the tower's radio waves, and invisible seepage from the Hexion Chemical plant, and casually speculated about the effect of these environmental hazards on a twelve-week-old fetus.

I saw Harold Benefield circle the Exxon parking lot in a tall white pickup truck and I waved. He'd driven directly from Butch's, the greasy spoon where he and my dad meet for runny eggs and coffee most Saturday mornings. I had emailed Judge Benefield to see if he could answer a few questions about the house on Barnett Road. According to the deeds, it was one of several properties tied to his family since the '30s. He suggested we meet for a tour instead.

The Judge, as my father called him, was a trim man approaching sixty. His Saturday outfit included squarish wireframe glasses and a black turtleneck tucked into jeans. Though we had both aged significantly since our last meeting, I suspected I still resemble a pigtailed toddler to my father's oldest friend. We spent almost no time on greetings.

"Let's start here," he said, striding toward the corner. "I was born in 1951."

I hurried to catch up and started jotting down his remarks. He detailed the structures and characters of all four corners of the intersection, from his grandfather's rental "flophouse" across the street to the inhabitants of the Town & Country mobile home park. His mother, Melba Barnette Benefield, had moved to this street in 1934, when she was fourteen.

"What about the trailer park?" I asked.

He shrugged. "That trailer park has been here forever."

We took a moment to marvel that the so-called "mobile" homes were the only enduring fixture on the block. It would be one of our few shared memories from our early years on Barnett Road.

"Every evening at 5 o'clock, I was allowed to walk down to this corner to wait for my father as he was coming home. He worked at the Ford plant in Hapeville." As the Judge told me this, he seemed to realize how odd it sounded that his mother had let him, the baby, the youngest of four boys, walk to the corner alone. If my dad allowed me to do that in the 1980s, he might have been arrested.

"There was very little regular traffic in those days," he continued. "Barnett Road was dirt until the early '60s."

There was very little traffic that day either. Old Dixie Highway was busy, but we were able to stand in the middle of Barnett Road and talk. I saw a grown man on a kid's bike looking at us as we walked slowly away from the corner. It was the same corner where I had scrapped my plan to run away from home.

The Judge continued to inventory the landscape, starting four miles north at the Ford plant, traveling down Old Dixie through the city limits of Mountain View and into Forest Park. He recalled P.D. Calloway's, a long-demolished country store that "smelled of salted mullet." It was here that he committed his first crime when he walked out with a box of Cracker Jack. Mrs. Benefield caught him snacking in the back seat of the car. She immediately returned to the store and made him surrender the stolen goods.

The "first time caught shoplifting" story is a staple of any walk down memory lane. I made a note of Calloway's, if only because it seemed superbly anachronistic for this strip of suburban asphalt. Instead of Zesto, the grimy fast food joint I remembered on that corner, I imagined a mercantile with farmhands whittling sticks out front. I don't think I have ever smelled salted mullet.

We walked west on Barnett Road, the spine of the road leading us gently uphill. The morning chill burned off and the sun warmed our backs as it crept overhead.

He described the Cahaba Motor Lodge, a 1940s era motel with a string of sweetheart cabins. He remembered the corner, and all kinds of nefarious acts committed there.

"Your dad said you must have been three when you moved here," he said. "I'm surprised you remember anything at all."

"How old were you when you got caught with the Cracker Jack?"

He paused to calculate.

"About three."

"You remember it, right?"

We kept walking. It had been a dry October, so the trees still had all their leaves, which rattled in place. Instead of "fall color" it just looked like an old photo with the cyan faded, leaving even the sky with a golden cast.

New stories cropped up every few yards and we stopped to discuss a tree, a curb, or a water tower. Like me, the Judge had a list of carnival memories of Barnett Road—the three-legged Irish setter on this corner, the guy with the golf-ball sized kidney stones across the street, Pa Barnette's hogs raised for sausage, a rumor about displaced Cuban diplomats in the trailer park. The adults probably noticed very little of this neighborhood surrealism.

"The south side of the street was always clear land," he said, pointing out a lot now occupied by bristly young pines and support sheds for the cell phone tower. There were cotton and cornfields during Melba Barnette's youth. Later on, the land was graded. The Judge mentioned that my grandfather taught my dad to drive in that field. I instantly pictured Grandaddy's pea-green Ford pickup lurching across the pasture, churning up clouds of red dirt, which is certainly a mashup of my own driving lessons with dad in another pickup truck in another field.

Each time a plane descended, I paused my note-taking so I could read the Judge's lips. Several times I completely lost track of what he was saying because of the noise. If only they could make the planes look cuter, less invading. Blunt their noses and round their windows and bellies so that they looked younger, more innocent and unsure, like wobbly cubs reaching out for a soft landing, and less like honed steel weapons aimed at the earth.

We strolled the length of the Town & Country. The mobile homes had sprouted roots—latticed foundations, carports, and porches. Several of the Easter egg-colored homes were clearly original to the complex. Judge Benefield pointed out the one where he first "beheld the mysteries of the female form" and another spot where a father routinely beat his children to "preempt them from sinning."

The Judge seemed to swing between boyish memories and adult perspective. I watched him closely to see which was which. He recalled his fascination when hobos and other nomads began building a village of shacks in the woods behind his house. And there were real live gypsies who trundled down the road in a horse and carriage, selling trinkets and asking for odd jobs. Parents warned that the gypsies would kidnap bad children at night. The young Judge sat on his front porch swing for hours watching for them. I wondered aloud if this was kind of a local boogey-man, but he was serious.

"It was all part of a new dynamic that came along when the Farmers Market opened," he said. "This area became a magnet for derelicts and drunks."

I'd never thought of the Farmers Market that way before. With its produce stalls and flower shops, it seemed like a benevolent place to me. It opened in 1959 and brought a huge boost of traffic, commerce, employment, and tropical fruit into Forest Park. It was the airport, I thought, that ruined Barnett Road.

"Did your parents have any idea that the Farmers Market would have that effect?"

I heard my own question hang in the air. It sounded pretty stupid. The Judge answered with a tidy summary of Atlanta history.

"No, they were up and comers, they were optimistic. At the time, Clayton County was the fastest growing county in the nation. They had all the cotton-picking they wanted."

Upgrading from a sixteen-acre site in Atlanta, the new Georgia State Farmers Market would be 146 acres in the booming suburb of Forest Park. Like the airport, the project was a huge commercial win for Clayton County, and a powerful example of how Atlanta's wealth, commerce, population—its center of gravity—was shifting to the white suburbs. The market would be the biggest open-air farmers market in the country, boasting spacious, modern stalls for farmers, plus wholesale warehouses, a cannery and a restaurant. It cost over ten million dollars to build, but this cost was offset, I learned, by generous tax breaks from the city of Forest Park.

"Farmers Market" always struck me as a misnomer. I worked in one of those produce warehouses the summer after high school, driving a forklift and assembling specialty produce orders for Atlanta restaurants. I never met a farmer. Instead, I met a colorful ensemble of truck drivers, lumpers, chefs and businessmen and spotted the occasional prostitute. The Georgia State Farmers Market was not a neighborhood-scale gathering place where local shoppers strolled among farm stands. It was an enormous transfer station off the freeway where shoppers drove up to loading docks, dodging semis and towers of pallets. While there were seasonal retail attractions like Christmas tree stalls, pumpkin patches, and watermelon festivals, this state agriculture facility has always functioned largely as a wholesale hub for a generation that celebrated shopping at supermarkets, not farmers markets.

The gritty side effects of "progress" were felt by the surrounding community almost immediately. The area had begun its transition to industrial usage. Within five years, the Barnettes began re-locating further south. The Judge was eight years old when the Farmers Market opened. He was fourteen when his family moved away.

We approached AirLogistics Center II, the long beige warehouse complex that had replaced the houses of Barnett Road. To the left, the land followed the grade of the road. To the right, where our houses would have been, the shoulder dropped eight feet to a retaining wall overlooking a parking lot. My tour guide estimated the location of where his father built their house in 1945. Next to that was the site of Granny and Pa Barnette's house. Beyond that was Uncle Alton and Aunt Ruby's house, the house I lived in. Then he stopped in the middle of the road.

"This is horrible," he said.

I scanned the horizon. Nothing moved. What was horrible?

"I can't help you see it. The level is so different." We were standing at the crest of Barnett Road where the driveway to Uncle Alton and Aunt Ruby's house used to be.

"This is the natural slope of the road," he said, gesturing to the left. "Reality existed on this level. And there were tall oak trees all around. It looks completely different now."

This was not the first time a man from my hometown assured me he could locate the place where he used to live. I watched the same scene with Rusty Stovall as he tried to find Morris Road in Mountain View. Disorientation, frustration, low-level alarm. No one expects the blankness. I have driven to this hill more than once and studied the backside of a warehouse for some clue in the angle of light, but the land itself has been reordered.

"I heard, I guess it was from Dad, that the fire department burned the house down as a training exercise."

The Judge frowned, thinking.

"Not that I recall. We sold it to your Dad's friend."

"Wendell Kitchens?"

"Right. The fellow with Superior Steel. I think they used one of the houses as an office for a while. Then they bulldozed this whole area. I came back over here and kicked through the wreckage. All I could find was a piece of tile that I recognized from my grandmother's bathroom."

The Judge would have been thirty years old during that little investigation. About my age. Somehow, a pile of rubble sounded even worse than ash. At least a training fire would have served a purpose.

He told me that he kept the tile for a while, but eventually lost it.

WHO WERE RUBY AND ALTON BARNETTE? I vaguely remembered them from their portrait in the church directory. They were even older than my grandparents—and had aged together and become shrunken and brown, like twin halves of a walnut.

They were married in 1935 and bought the house next door to Granny and Pa Barnette. This information came from an index card the Judge produced from his back pocket.

Aunt Ruby stood out in his memories as a brittle character. A gifted gardener and quilter, she was also unpredictably angry and prone to tears.

"Woe unto the child that touched her flowers," he said. "She acted like you killed someone."

There were daffodils that I used to gather by the handful all spring. Surely Ruby had planted the bulbs. Another piece of the puzzle snapped into place.

"She could be unkind to my mother, and to my grandmother, well…" And he left it at that.

We had finally arrived at the point on our walk and in the story that I was most interested in hearing, but the Judge turned around and started walking back down the hill. He was moving at such a pace that I began to think I had kept him too long, or struck a nerve.

We had almost reached the Exxon station when I made a comment

about how entertaining it must have been to grow up next door to all
his cousins.

"They were all much older. So were my brothers," he said. "And
Alton and Ruby were childless."

That word stopped me in my tracks. "They were?"

"And I imagine that might have had something to do with
her...unhappiness," he said.

Childless. The entire book of Ruby Barnette fell open before me.
After my own failed pregnancies, I had an inkling of that pervasive
"unhappiness," whole years that I wanted to erase. To be married
and childless in the 1940s and '50s, for whatever reason, must have
been a near biblical affliction. In vitro fertilization—the radical hope
of every thwarted would-be parent—was decades away from reality.
And if the Barnettes made the choice not to have kids, Forest Park
was quite possibly the worst place to attempt a progressive lifestyle.
Young families were on every side, Melba Benefield next door with
four boys. Kids ruled every patch of vacant grass. The entire city, with
its tidy subdivisions, top-notch schools, baseball diamonds, football
fields, and scout huts, was designed for breeding. It seemed possible
that it could make a woman miserable.

Back at the truck, the Judge laid a couple photo albums on the
tailgate and began flipping through them. He had selected a few that
showed the houses in the late '50s. He handed me a square black and
white photo of a boy on a bicycle, a cousin or a neighbor, he wasn't
sure. The boy was sitting in a dirt driveway, leaning back in the seat,
hands loosely holding the handlebars. His expression was annoyed,
or maybe he was just squinting into the sun. The pecan trees behind
him were theatrically lit. The shadow of three adults, one of whom is
holding the camera, stretched to fill the left side of the composition.

"That's Ruby and Alton's house," he said.

It was there in the background, tall and white and really nothing
like I remembered. I almost objected, but I recognized the light. I was
not mistaken about the lengthening effect it had on our shadows.

At last I was holding a photo of the house, but I felt even more lost. The perspective was off. Ruby and Alton passed away and left no descendants, no one to tell me their real story. No one with a photo album of their Christmases in the living room or Ruby's flowerbeds in bloom. I could scan the photo at high resolution and zoom in on the faded, blurry house in the background, but it wouldn't help. The information wasn't there.

Forest Park Fire Department Training Burn,
Department of Public Safety, 1982.

FOURTEEN

FIREHOUSES

“There was a motel on the corner,” said Chief Buckholts when I asked him what he remembered about Barnett Road.

I had walked into the Forest Park Fire and EMS Services headquarters politely hoping to find a record of burn exercises, a list of houses that might include my house on Barnett Road. Instead, a stocky, round-faced captain who looked to be not much older than I, ushered me back to the chief's office. He led me down a dim cinderblock hallway, through a long room lined with twin beds, tightly wrapped in burgundy coverlets.

Eddie Buckholts, the fire chief, turned slowly to greet me, as if it caused him physical pain. He was a large man in his late fifties, wearing a starched white Fire Department shirt with spiky white hair to match. He didn't get up from his chair.

"The Cahaba Motor Lodge?" I offered. I had just learned of its existence.

"And now it's the Hexion plant," he said. Not a question, but a statement of fact. The firemen, I quickly learned, knew every structure and every street corner in the city intimately. It made sense that in order to assess fire risk, they would be aware of the age, construction, and general activities within the buildings around town. Still, I was impressed. Why did I waste all that time looking at deed books? Buckholts grew up in Forest Park and worked for the fire service for his entire career. Like the Sanborn maps, the fire insurance maps that provide some of the earliest and most thorough documentation of American cities, he was a living, breathing atlas of the city.

I introduced myself and threw in the maiden name, my favorite trick.

"Are you any kin to Bobby Slagle?"

Here we go, I thought. "He's my uncle."

"He was one of the fastest running backs to ever come out of the state of Georgia," said the chief, more to the captain than to me.

Fastest in the state? I shared what little I knew of Uncle Bobby's short-lived but legendary football career. My dad's brother passed up a football scholarship to study art and his football days were long behind him.

"So did you play football with him?" I asked, turning the question back to the chief.

"Actually, it goes deeper than that," he said. "He was the reason why we moved to Forest Park. I grew up in Valdosta, and we played them in 1968. I was thirteen years old."

"Wait, he was the reason?"

He explained how the state championship game coincided with his father's plans to move the family to the Atlanta area for work. They were searching for a nice neighborhood near Atlanta, and that game against the Panthers, led by Bobby Slagle, formed their first impression of Forest Park. It seemed to his father that if a team was good enough to come all the way down to Valdosta, a football powerhouse at the farthest end of Georgia, then it had to be a good enough school for his son. They moved to Clayton County the next year.

I had to admit, it was as good as any reason to choose a neighborhood. The Forest Park Panther football team was just one emblem of a school system in its prime. During the '50s and '60s, the Clayton County schools were a model for the state, even the nation. The county boasted modern new schools and stadiums. Strong athletics were matched by academics and arts. The thriving marching band, the Miss Forest Park Pageant, the Key Club, the Junior ROTC—all the vital signs were strong. My parents' yearbooks are hundreds of pages thick with local advertisers, clubs, and page after page of smiling, white faces. Boys with matching crewcuts, girls with orange juice can curls. The schools remained racially segregated until 1969, with the African-American kids funneled to Fountain High School near Rosetown.

The schools could barely keep up with the baby boomers. From 1953 to 1973, the population of Forest Park tripled. The suburban county absorbed waves of white flight as Atlanta began integrating its schools in 1962. Employers such as the Ford Assembly plant, Fort Gillem, Eastern Airlines, Delta Airlines, and other airport support industries attracted blue-collar WWII vets from every corner of the Southeast. My grandparents followed a similar migration from agricultural regions to industrial jobs on the southside.

By 1995, the sprawling Metro Atlanta area had an equally sprawling smog problem to contend with. Clayton County became part of the thirteen-county "Ozone Nonattainment Area," subject to strict new rules for air quality control. EPA regulations mandated a ban on open fires from May through September, and fire departments were tasked with issuing fire permits based on daily fire conditions. The same rules severely restricted controlled burns by fire departments. Any structure to be burned had to be stripped of asbestos, fiberglass, shingles, most metals, and other common building materials. It became too costly to conduct training exercises within the city limits. In effect, training burns in Clayton County became a thing of the past.

I asked about the last of the training burns in Forest Park.

"That was in 1994," the captain said wistfully, "That was my rookie burn."

"Is that the one where we had smoke on the Parkway?" asked the chief, "We had to shut down Forest Parkway at five o'clock in the evening."

"The wind changed up on us!"

They described a burn near Phillips Drive, where the CVS is now. I realized they were reminiscing about the one and only burn exercise I have attended, when I was teenager in Forest Park. It was the little yellow stucco house behind our house on Phillips Drive.

"I have a video of it somewhere," he said.

Of course they made videos, I thought. They reviewed them just like football games—for training. I've watched a few of these "instructional" burn videos on YouTube. One had a Metallica soundtrack, the other used a medley of Slipknot hits. My hopes were growing that there was some kind of formal documentation of my house, some well-worn photos tucked away like beloved porn.

"Do you think anyone would remember the burn on Barnett Road?" I asked.

They debated for a minute about who served in the '80s and then abruptly radioed Station 2 and asked for Sergeant Earles.

"There's a lady here, doing research. Wants to know about a training burn over on Barnett Road," the chief said.

After a brief pause, a voice crackled through the device.

"I remember doing it but that's been too long ago. I've probably done twenty or thirty of them." I stared at the blinking green light of the transmitter, incredulous.

"You sure you done it?" the chief asked. "It was this lady's family home."

"I know we done it," the voice continued. "That's when they started clearing out behind Martin Burks."

I was nodding involuntarily at the device. Martin Burks Chevrolet was the dealership on the other side of Barnett Road, next to the Zesto.

"It was sitting in a bunch of old oak trees," he said.

With that remark, I was convinced. Even if that was all he remembered, it was still more evidence than I had been able to find in all the deed books, tax maps, and newspaper archives of Clayton County.

A FEW DAYS LATER, I met the man who burned down my house. Sgt. Mike Earles was one of a whole battalion of firemen who participated in the training burn on Barnett Road. The Forest Park Fire Department burned three or four structures on the street, as he remembered it. With drills for extrications, bridging walls, and search and rescue, it took a week to complete the burn.

"Well, it wasn't your house," he said, laughing, as I explained my investigation.

"No, it was Georgia Power's by then."

I didn't bother to mention that it was never legally my house. I don't think my dad even paid rent. It was just a place where I spent a few years of my childhood. This was my first clue that Earles wasn't one for sentimentality. Torching houses was just a part of the job. It was possible that I envied this about him.

I had interrupted a training class and Earles stepped out to take a cigarette break with me. He checked for fire ants before perching on the steps. He was only too happy to step out of his class.

"EMT stuff," he said, with a dismissive wave.

Silver hair under his FPFD cap, uniform tight around his midsection, he looked every bit the career fireman. His face and forearms were leathery and brown, as if smoked. Again, I was seated across from a Forest Park boy in his mid-fifties, a man who reminded me of my father.

He tried lighting a Marlboro in the wind. We sat on the cinder block stairs behind Fire Station 2 on an exceptionally warm and gusty afternoon. Dry leaves flickered as they blew from tree to tree. I could see fire hazards everywhere, even though the summer-long ban on open burns had just been lifted.

Station 2 was situated behind Ash Street Elementary, where I attended kindergarten and first grade. There was a wooden storage shed and a three-story training tower behind the brick station. Extension ladders and rappelling equipment leaned against the glassless windows. I told Earles that I remembered eyeing the fire station, particularly that training tower, from the playground with fascination.

"That's not the tower you remember," he said. "It was over there. We had to tear it down and build a new one."

He would know. He'd been with the fire department since 1971. A native of Thomaston, a small town near Macon, Georgia, Earles joined the fire service not long after he dropped out of Robert E. Lee High School.

"We played Forest Park in football, do you remember?"

I did not. But I started wondering how many of the football players from my high school days found a career as firemen. It seems like a natural continuation of team-oriented machismo, with good benefits and a pension. I asked what brought him to the Atlanta area.

"I didn't want to work in a cotton mill, which was all we had in Thomaston." He had to relight his cigarette, which had extinguished as he talked. "I knew about the Farmers Market. My first job was at the grocery store, and once a week I had to drive up here to pick up produce."

There wasn't much to say about the training burn on Barnett Road. He described a couple of houses like Alton and Ruby's and Guy and Melba's, each with a small garage apartment out back. It was a routine exercise, memorable only because of the risk posed by those giant oaks. Before the rules changed, Earles recalled taking part in training fires in Forest Park every six months. From his first burn on Glade Road, where he got his ears blistered, there were more than thirty houses over the years. It wasn't just a part of the job, but his favorite part of the job.

"We loved it," he said fondly. "We used to knock out the windows, cut holes in the roof. We set fires with pine straw or wheat straw, just to smoke it up for the search and rescue."

I pinched a fire ant just as it bit me under my wedding ring. Now fighting fires is only a small part of his job. Medical emergencies account for 70 percent of calls to the station. In 1992 the department officially updated its name to "Forest Park Fire and EMS Services." Burn exercises are no longer a method for clearing blighted houses. They are tightly controlled events at the Georgia Fire Academy in south Georgia.

"It used to be a lot calmer around here. It was more laid back. I lived on Burks Road for seventeen years before I moved out of Clayton."

His house was in a neighborhood directly in the path of the airport runways.

"Only reason I bought that house was to get the airport to buy it from me," he said. "Like they done in Mountain View."

I grinned at his bluntness. "But they quit buying out homeowners, didn't they?"

"They bought the air rights," he said. "They come through and did the insulation, new windows and doors, siding, central heat and air."

"So you stayed?"

He tried to blow smoke away from me, but the wind carried it back.

"After seventeen years, a place becomes home. You get used to it."

I remembered conversations among classmates about when they were going to move. It was inevitable. Many families held out to be acquired by the airport as their neighbors sold their houses for a loss, or to developers. As the noise level grew, the property values dropped.

"Eventually, I had to let it go for nothing."

IMPRESSED AT THE RECORDKEEPING of the fire department, I left a message with the tiny Forest Park Museum of History and asked for an appointment to view their collection of Fire Department memorabilia. The "museum" had been organized just two years earlier, as part of the citywide centennial celebration.

The museum was housed in the old Scout Hut, a small, no-frills cinder block building on the grounds of the Forest Park Recreation Center. From second grade to middle school, I spent practically every Monday night there for Girl Scout troop meetings. I recited the pledge in one room, sorted cases of cookies in another, painted banners, rehearsed skits, and built a camp oven out of aluminum foil and coat hangers in the parking lot of that building. I was giddy to share all this with the city employee from Support Services who was waiting for me on the porch in the pouring rain.

Before I even shook out my umbrella, we recognized each other. Beverly Martin was a name and a face I knew from Jones Memorial Methodist. She was twenty years older, but her diminutive features, long dark hair, and freckled nose were unmistakable.

"Miss Slagle! I didn't know I was coming to meet you," she said. "The appointment said some other name."

Only in Forest Park, Georgia, would the name "Slagle" ring any bells. We hugged. I'm shorter than average and Martin only came up to my shoulder.

We spent a moment catching up as she unlocked the front door and punched in an alarm code. I felt like skipping into the place. The interior was as I remembered it, only less cluttered. The clean vinyl tile floors and cinder block walls were lit from above by the same cheap linear fluorescents. A recent coat of beige paint brightened the rooms and masked any memory-triggering smells. Outside, rain was beating on the roof and the sky darkened. I felt like a tornado could tear through Forest Park and this low, blocky hut would keep us safe.

"I used to go to Girl Scouts here!" I said.

"Really? This building is about to be torn down," she said, wiping at her wet sleeves.

"It is?"

"Probably next year," she said. "It's just old and drafty. The ceiling is falling in."

I sighed and looked at the place again. The rooms were small and uninsulated. There were water stains on the ceiling tiles. It was probably built, as cheaply as possible, in the late '6os and wasn't worth restoring.

I guess she saw the disappointment on my face. "Well, you know they tore down most of Main Street for the new train station."

"Right." Same old story.

"Supposedly, they'll move all this to a room in the new train station," she said, gesturing towards the standing exhibits and binders of the museum. "But it'll just be something you walk through and look at. There won't be anyone there to tell you stories."

We started with a wall dedicated to Forest Park's mayors, and she told me stories about the mayors. This one was an undertaker, another was an accountant, and that one was a crook. Then we moved to the police and fire department display. An old set of boots and a helmet from 1955 were preserved under a Plexiglass cube. The opposite wall included a city map from 1904, snapshots of a greased pig contest in the '70s, and a series of black-and- white class photos from city schools. It was an oddly entertaining mix.

"This one's a sad story," Martin said as I peered at a photo on the wall. Instead of the normal class photo, where children were herded onto bleachers or into lines, in this photo, they were seated with their hands folded on their desks, grinning sweetly at the camera. It had a handwritten tag that said: "Lake City Elem. Mrs. Haines 3rd Grade 1959-60."

"The city manager found it at a yard sale on Patricia Drive," she began. "The folks had died and their sons just didn't-care, they were selling everything."

I lost track of what she was saying because a boy on the front row had my attention. His tilted smile resembled my little brother at that age. The eyes looked like mine. I gasped and planted my finger on the glass of the photo.

"That's my Dad!"

She stepped closer to take a look.

"Sure enough," she said with a laugh. "All the Slagle boys were good-looking."

The longer I stared at it, the more familiar the scene became. The room with its chalkboard, corner closets, and long coat rack looked exactly like my third grade classroom. I even recognized Judge Harold Benefield, age eight, in the back row. The kid that was so obviously my crewcut, snaggle-toothed father, leaned forward and smiled right at me. Why hadn't I noticed him immediately? I felt a surge of protective recognition and love that I can only compare to the feeling of seeing my own son take shape on a black-and-white ultrasound screen. Dad's shiny black shoes barely touched the floor under his desk.

I took a photo of the photo. I pondered it as we moved to another wall of black-and-white scenes. As much as I treasured that glimpse of my dad, it seemed completely random. Why was it here? Why that particular third grade class? I had to wonder about the criteria for inclusion in this museum. How old does something have to be before it qualifies as historic? This old building wasn't deemed worthy of preservation; neither was Main Street. I later learned that the photo appeared in the *Clayton News Daily* to commemorate the inaugural class at Lake City Elementary. It was an artifact of the county's explosive mid-century expansion, but the Museum of History didn't know that—they just found it at a yard sale. The walls were like a haphazard memorial for everything that has been demolished and everyone who has moved away.

Finally, Martin led me to a binder of photos contributed by the Fire Department. I was expecting snapshots of retirement ceremonies, but once again, I had underestimated these guys. Instead I found sleeve after sleeve of dramatic full page, professional quality, black-and-white photos documenting training burns in the early 1980s. Each one was dated and stamped on the back with "Forest Park Department of Public Safety."

The photographer clearly had an artist's eye for detail. Some of the shots were breathtaking—frills of smoke emerging from the eaves of a collapsing house, a stray grocery cart on the porch, fully engulfed in white flames, the geometric grid of ladders and water spray high above a smoldering roofline. Many of the photos, enlarged and art-fully framed, could hang in a gallery or in my living room.

Martin was able to identify a few of the locations, and we agreed that they were some of the loveliest old houses the city ever condemned. As I paged through 1982, 1983, and 1984, my heart rate increased. I scrutinized each porch and driveway for signs that it might be mine.

"Now which house are you looking for?" she asked. "Was it the one I used to babysit you at?"

I tried not to look startled. She had been my babysitter? The cura-tor of the Forest Park Museum of History?

"When was this?" I asked.

"Long time ago," she said. "Your parents were still married."

That narrowed it down to the house in Mountain View, not the one on Barnett Road. She had probably changed my diapers thirty years ago. Small world.

One of the last photos in the binder was a training burn of an anony-mous white house in 1985. The date, the style of the house, the tall oak trees around it, and the corner of a garage at the end of a long driveway were enough to make me break out in a sweat. I slid the photo out of its plastic sleeve and studied it for a long time. Could this be my lost house, with black smoke and flames pouring out of the windows?

The rain was slowing down outside and my head hurt. I took a photo of the photo and packed up my camera.

Later on at home, I would compare this house with the one in the photo from the Benefield family album. The pitch of the roof was right, but the position of the chimney was wrong. It was like reading a horoscope—parts of the image fit with my memory of the place, but others were a stretch. Neither photo was a satisfying match with the house in my mind.

I considered showing the photo to my father or to Judge Benefield, but decided that would be bizarre, even morbid. I might legitimately ask, Is this our old house? But it would feel more like, Hi Dad, does this scene of destruction tear open any old wounds?

As Beverly switched off the lights, I offered to sign the museum guest book.

"It doesn't really matter," she said.

She was just being expedient, but the comment made me uneasy. I had this bleak feeling that our afternoon together was more than a series of coincidences. The old Scout Hut, past its expiration date, was left standing for our brief encounter. And here were the exact photos I needed, rescued and stored in a place where no one would ever look for them. It all could have been staged for me specifically, an elaborate set-up. And now that I was leaving, it could all be torn down behind me, as soon as I drove away.

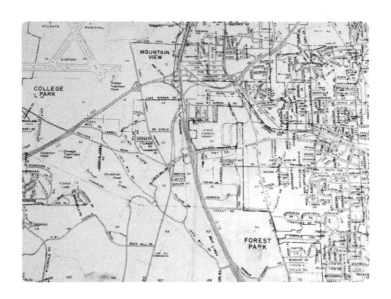

Large scale wall map at Jones Memorial United Methodist Church.

FIFTEEN

NAMES

At Jones Memorial United Methodist Church, the holiday season officially began with the United Methodist Women's Christmas Tea. Typically set for the first Saturday in December, this annual ladies luncheon had evolved into a combination year-end assembly, church homecoming, and the prime opportunity to publicly display granddaughters and fine china. Ladies signed up to "sponsor" each of the round, ten-seat tables, and decorated them with their own unique Christmas theme and holiday finery.

This year I was invited to sit at Gayle's table—the Peppermint Table. I pulled a wool, houndstooth skirt up over my expanding waistline and covered up in a loose gray sweater, silently praying that my maternity wear would pass church-lady approval.

In the years since I moved away to college, I have returned to the church a dozen or so times for baby and bridal showers and to attend the annual Christmas Tea. One summer, in an explosion of hometown loyalty and affection, Jason and I were married here. With each visit, I felt more and more self-conscious about "leaving" the church. Located on Phillips Drive, between my third house and Lake City Elementary, the place consistently satisfied my need for a stable home base. The brick red floor tiles underfoot, the echoing voices in the

Fellowship Hall, all of it was unchanged from the time I was a flower girl in Dad and Gayle's wedding in 1984 to my own wedding in 2002.

On our way down to Forest Park, Jason and I stopped at the State Farmers Market to buy a Christmas tree. We parked the truck at the end of a long, open pavilion crowded with Western North Carolina firs and strolled into the makeshift forest to make our decision. Between the Palmer family tradition of hacksawing down a tree each year at a nearby tree farm, and my family's reliance on an artificial tree hoisted down from the attic each November, the Farmers Market was our compromise. Our negotiating process had been tested over the years since we moved back to Georgia and started putting up a tree—I preferred the bushy Leland Cypress; he liked the spiky Fraser Firs. The tree could be small, modest, and imperfect, but we both agreed, it had to be local, or at least relatively local.

The tree should look like a tree, I told the tree farm guy. Not too perfect, nothing trendy. A real Southern Pine.

And so we zigzagged through the fragrant tree lot for half an hour, knowing that they all look the same after a while. The white sky pressed down on the acres of pavement, muffling the hidden airplanes overhead.

This negotiation was not unlike our ongoing search for baby names. We joked about names like Santiago and Thor, many syllables or just one. But they sounded too exotic. I threw out any rootless, made-up names. My friends picked cowboy wannabe names like Cody, Jackson, and Dakota. Others tried to elevate their social class with names like Brayden, Cole, and Greyson. I decreed that it should be a family name or a name with a meaningful story. Then again, history could be a burden. Bible names like Samuel and Gideon were too loaded. I had so many rules and no idea where they all came from.

The kid would need to sound authentic, like he came from someplace, specifically from here. I mentally noted names while perusing the deed books of the last hundred years of Clayton County. Clark, Alton, Wade, Gus, or Henry. Before the 1950s, men's names often appeared as initials, like O.K. Sellers, B.C. Haynie, or D.M. Harrison. I suppose it was a way to curb irregular spelling.

Eventually, we settled on a seven-foot Fraser Fir with an uneven top and a mild citrus scent. We strapped our bundle in the back of the truck and Jason dropped me off at the church.

The Fellowship Hall was packed with poinsettias and red-sweatered women. A Mannheim Steamroller CD was playing behind a Christmas tree adorned with hand-knit items for the homeless shelter. Among the crowd of familiar faces were Beverly Martin and Melba Benefield.

At this point, my belly was beginning to introduce itself. As I greeted each of the grand dames of my childhood, I wavered at their perfumed perimeter and answered the standard round of questions: How far along are you? Do you know what you're having? Do you have a name picked out? It was nice to be part of the club, to have something to talk about. These are the same ladies, I thought, who cooed over my mom when she was pregnant with me. I honed my response with each happy repetition: five months, a boy, we haven't decided yet. Should I tell Mrs. Benefield, I wondered, that the name at the top of our list was Guy, that I was inspired by the name of her late husband I read on a deed?

Gayle sent me over to the Evergreen table to say hello. Mrs. Melba was in her eighties and didn't try to stand to embrace me. She wore wide glasses that magnified her large, watery eyes and made her look even more like the Judge. Her hair was a fine white cloud. I leaned over her shoulder to hear her over the din of conversation in the hall.

"Harold told me about your morning together," she said. I smiled to hear "the Judge" referred to as Harold. "He thoroughly enjoyed it."

I wanted to quiz her about her sister-in-law Ruby Barnette. Why was the house deeded to Ruby from her husband in 1948? Why didn't they have any children?

Instead, I asked, "Who was Barnett Road named after? And why isn't it "Barnette" with an "e"?"

She chuckled. "Somebody misspelled it. It was named after my family, they just lost the "e" somewhere."

Then the president of the United Methodist Women started her announcements and I had to make my way back to Gayle's table. I felt like the morning was already a success because Mrs. Melba had set me straight on the names.

THEN THERE WAS THE Flournoys' approach to baby names. The family who lived next door to my grandparents in Forest Park had a houseful of kids, each of them named after a character from *Gone With the Wind*. From the oldest—Rhett—to the youngest and only girl—Scarlett—and all the boys in between. Even as a kid I found it dangerously cheesy and fanatical to give exclusive naming rights for all your kids to a single book, unless maybe it was the Bible. But I liked the idea of a name from literature, especially if the book was a local treasure.

Rhett and Ashley were much older, already in high school, the youngest and only girl was Scarlett, but Cade was my age. He grew up to be an all-around hottie, good at everything he tried from football to musical theater. And Cade, I thought, was a pretty cool name. What about Cade Palmer?

It was for that reason, and nothing more scholarly, that I picked up a copy of *Gone With the Wind* for the first time when I was six months pregnant. How is it that I never read it before? How could a Clayton County native, an English major and self-professed lover of Southern Lit, have escaped reading this book? As a literary tourist, I had visited Margaret Mitchell's apartment on Peachtree Street, her grave in Oakland Cemetery, and the corner by the state Capitol where she was struck by a car while crossing the road.

Clayton County is dotted with Taras and Twelve Oaks, making it hard to tell the real places that inspired Mitchell from modern replicas. A Vivien Leigh look-alike in a green-and-white hoop skirt ensemble

made appearances at community functions. Our geographic identity
was so steeped in the mystique of Tara, it never occurred to me to
read the book. But I couldn't name my son after Cade Flournoy, the
kid I barely knew from Shellnut Drive; it had to be the Cade from
Gone With the Wind. What kind of character was he? I had to read
the novel.

Jason and I spent the first blank days of the new year snowed in
at home. Between de-Christmasing the house and pondering the
nursery, I curled up on the sofa with the dog and Margaret Mitchell's
masterpiece. In the back of my mind, I warned myself that novels get
attached to the time and place they are read. Starting this book, at
this time, would elevate it to The Book I Was Reading While I Was
Pregnant. How would a Civil War-era romance affect the baby? I rea-
soned that reading *Gone With the Wind* would be much more fun than
the other books I got for Christmas: Franklin Garrett's three-volume
history *Atlanta and Environs* and Ina May Gaskin's *Birthing From
Within.* Jason dragged the tree to the backyard to burn it, leaving a
short trail of dry pine needles from the living room to the back door.

"What's that book about anyways?" he asked. I told him I was
looking for baby names.

In some ways, the novel was exactly what I expected—a juicy
love story. The sexual tension between the swarthy, dashing Rhett
Butler and headstrong heroine Scarlett O'Hara fuels the whole story.
I cheered over lines like: "He bowed and sauntered off, leaving her
with her bosom heaving with impotent rage and indignation." The
same level of melodrama is there when Papa O'Hara says, "Do you
mean to tell me, Katie Scarlett O'Hara, that Tara, that land doesn't
mean anything to you? The land is the only thing in the world worth
working for, worth fighting for, worth dying for, because it's the only
thing that lasts."

Maybe because of this line from the movie, I had the notion that
Tara, the white-columned plantation house, had been around forever.
That it symbolized, in fact, the enduring Old South. On the contrary,

O'Hara built Tara on the ruined foundation of another burnt house just a few years before the action of the story began. When the plantation is sacked by Union troops, Scarlett is still a young woman. Tara couldn't have been more than three decades old—that's far younger than any of my lost houses, which survived forty, fifty and sixty-seven years. Even my house in Mountain View, carted off to make way for the airport, lasted longer than Tara.

I was surprised by the compression of time, Atlanta's short history. Scarlett takes pride in the fact that she was born in 1847, the same year that Atlanta was christened. Her lifetime encapsulates the whole story of the birth, burning, and rebuilding of the city. In the same way, the timeline of my life could be the same as that of the new airport. I was born at the same time as Atlanta's aspirations to become an international city, and I grew up along with the city's awkward adolescent identity crisis.

The cast of characters included many delicious names: Raphael Semmes (a Confederate naval admiral), Solange Robillard (Scarlett's grandmother), Dilcey and Pork (slaves at Tara), Maybelle Merriwether, Pittypat Hamilton, India Wilkes, and Carreen O'Hara. Cade Calvert was a minor character. He's a privileged son of a Clayton County planter and one of our heroine's many beaux who returns from the war demoralized and withered with tuberculosis. Cade dies, a symbol of youth and potential squandered. Beyond that, he's not much more than a name.

Though *Gone With the Wind* could've ended two hundred pages earlier, I diligently slogged through its prickly denouement. I had to keep reading. It felt like the hazing ritual of a very special Southern sorority. When baby kicks and anxiety kept me awake at 3:00 AM and 4:00AM, I curled up with the huge novel on my belly. There was the sense of having outlasted *Gone With the Wind*, having wrestled through my pregnancy-induced insomnia with Scarlett O'Hara and the character I wished she would become. When it was finished, I could take my place at the Christmas Tea with Gayle, Mrs. Melba, and Beverly Martin, the ladies of the United Methodist Women, and all the Clayton County matriarchs. I was beginning to imagine the losses they had sustained.

SIXTEEN

AS GOOD A PLACE
AS ANY

Perhaps you, like me, have puzzled over what leads an ordinary person to become a developer. Do they go through some kind of formal training in city planning or business? Or are young developers groomed, like artists and athletes, by families with an established record in the field? Real estate developers are a misunderstood, often faceless breed, only slightly better defined than the ominous "they." As in, "Looks like they're building something over there."

Who is they? Even when you dig deeper, it's hard to identify some responsible party. The developer is frequently not a person, but a corporation concocted for an isolated project. The layers of shell corporations can be numbingly complex, as each corporate entity distances itself from liability. In the end, no one's name is on the paperwork. It's hard to find a human developer.

So I was curious to talk with L.C. Cole, a retired fire chief who paired his long career with the Forest Park Fire Department with a profitable hobby or "sideline" buying, moving, selling, and renting houses from the airport area. In theory, that makes him a developer. The more I asked firemen about my lost houses, the more I heard his name. He seemed like my best chance for finding out what had happened to the houses of Mountain View.

When we first spoke on the phone, Cole didn't think he'd have any insight to share. "I don't know anything about Mountain View as far as that's concerned," he said. He downplayed any knowledge of the political "shiftiness" that eventually led to the revocation of the city's charter. Fair enough, I thought. I had long accepted that no one wanted to testify on what went down in that sorry episode. Instead, I asked about the construction work he used to do on the side.

"I did move a good many houses," he said. "Mostly from the airport area when they was expanding back then. Most of the property that I moved out was where the runways are now."

While the people of Mountain View can be found reuniting on Facebook, it has proven much harder to track the diaspora of the city's structures. I told Cole I'd like to hear more about the houses that he moved. I offered to meet him practically anywhere, anytime. "I still have some rental properties in the Forest Park area," he said. "I go up there pretty often."

After at least five phone calls, in which I awkwardly spelled and re-spelled my name for him, in which I learned that Cole was significantly hearing-impaired, we finally found a time to meet. He suggested the Forest Park Fire Department headquarters as location for the interview. "It's as good a place as any," he said.

I PULLED UP IN THE parking lot on a clear, sunny afternoon in late winter. It was a day for sunglasses, a day that reminds you why people migrate to Atlanta—mid-February, high-fifties temperatures. Rubbery daffodil nubs were poking up around the flagpole. I cruised through the small lot, wondering what kind of vehicle might be driven by a retired fire chief, a developer, and quite possibly, the man who moved my house. Maybe the late '90s, red GMC truck with "disabled veteran" tags? I parked next to it. A tiny black dog leapt into the driver's side window and launched into a muffled tirade.

One of the firemen spotted me crossing the parking lot and opened a side door. They were expecting me. He motioned me directly into the break room where a half dozen men were mid-lunch and chatting with Cole. He was the only one out of uniform, but he still commanded the room. A tall, broad-shouldered man in his late seventies, he wore brown slacks, a scuffed bomber jacket, gold-framed glasses, and a hearing aid. His thick silver hair was combed back with Brilliantine. Everyone milled around the microwave and the television while he stood by the black-tinted window, watching.

I felt the distinct self-consciousness of being the only woman in the room. I wore my bulging pregnant belly like an inappropriate outfit; it felt almost confrontational. Cole introduced himself with a quiet handshake. He briskly guided me through the cinder block hallway, through the room lined with thin beds, to a cluttered, private office at the back of the building. The smell of toasted Wonder bread wafted along behind us.

As I started asking about his thirty-year history with the fire service, Cole leaned forward to hear me better. Twice within our first ten minutes in the office, we paused when firemen stopped by to greet the former chief. "I heard you were here," they said, brimming with admiration. "Don't mean to interrupt."

If Cole enjoyed the attention, he was reserved about it.

"See those boards?" he said, when the last visitor left. He pointed at row of black felt menu boards above the desk with white letters spelling out the names of the firemen on each shift. "There's probably only three or four fellows on each board that I hired. I used to know all of them, 'cause I hired them."

It took me a minute to see where he was going with this. All the names were unknown to me, but to him, the boards were a familiar sight, slightly altered. Like someone snuck in and rearranged the books on his shelf.

I asked him if he missed it. I tried to get a look at his brassy watch, wondering what a top level fireman gets for thirty-four years of service. He said he could have retired sooner, but he wasn't ready.

"I know some chiefs, they retire and sit at home with the radio on, listening," he said. "Then they chase the trucks out on a call. They can't let it go." The fire service, he explained, was not the kind of career that people pursued for the money, or the pension. It was a way of life, a calling, all of which made it harder to give it up.

"If I had left too early, that would've been me too. But I was ready." He planned to use his free time to look after his rental properties.

Cole seemed uncomfortable with the idea that I might consider him an expert on Mountain View. He was born and raised in Blue Ridge, a small mountain town in north Georgia. After high school and military service, he settled in Miami in 1950 and ended up working for Pan Am (or "Pan American World Airways," as he said it). He landed in a good spot. His small house near the airport was the start of his good fortune. It was an area that was rapidly developing and he was able to sell his house at enough profit to reinvest in more properties. He discovered a knack for real estate.

"When we moved back to Georgia, they were clearing out for the airport. I picked up where I left off."

That was 1960. I told him I had been trying to piece together the general fate of the houses of Mountain View, in hopes that I would find a clue about my old house on South West Street. I told him about my track record with old houses—two demolished, two moved to locations unknown.

"I may have one of them," he said amiably. I cringed.

"How did you get them?"

He walked me through the transfer of ownership from individual homeowners to the City of Atlanta, which paid full price for the properties, then sold the structures to a house mover. By the time he came into the picture, the houses were being auctioned off in large quantities. "The house mover might have fifty of them. They weren't sold individually."

I pictured a vast field of houses on wheels, like a used car lot. Jason told me he remembered looking out the back windows of the family van in the early '80s on trips to Chick-fil-A. The Palmers drove through Mountain View on the way from Conley to Hapeville. He remembered the eerie sight of house after house jacked up on flatbed trailers.

"The houses were still on location," said Cole. "Sometimes people still lived in them."

How did he decide which houses were worth relocating? How does any developer know what the market will support? Cole told me about one quirky "development" that brought him particular pride. Sometime in the mid '70s, he acquired a group of Mountain View houses at auction and had them relocated to a semi-rural lot south of the airport. The tiny brick houses—no longer up to code in Clayton County—were a bargain. As fire chief, he had an intimate knowledge of building codes, so he got creative. He placed houses together in pairs to make a whole neighborhood of duplexes.

Instant slum! I thought, as he described the project with a crafty grin. Cheap houses mashed together must be worth even less than the sum of their parts. Especially now that the airport had its new massive runway slicing across the top of Clayton County, I expected the neighborhood had become a noisy, neglected, dead-end street, dotted with weedy, abandoned duplexes.

"So is there any way to track down a particular house?" I asked. "I mean, there are deeds on the land, but not the houses. Do you think the house movers kept track of where houses ended up?"

I grilled Cole with cheery courtesy. Hearing my own questions out loud, I had to admit the quest seemed farfetched. A structure, disconnected from the land, is hard to value and hard to trace.

The interviewer, I thought, shouldn't do this much talking. But I pressed on. "I've looked for city contracts with the house movers, but they aren't required to keep thirty-year-old records. And if there aren't records, my best bet is to ask people like you who remember. I've called the house movers, but they aren't inclined to talk with me. So how else am I supposed to find my old house?"

He was smiling patiently, leaning forward.

"That would be near impossible," he said.

It occurred to me that his look of concentration was more likely a sign of lip-reading than genuine concern.

"Did you ever get attached to a house?" I asked.

"No, I guess not," Cole chuckled. "Not so much I couldn't let go of it if I needed to."

What more could I say? I thanked him for his help. And it was, in fact, profoundly helpful to be told by this modest, yet authoritative, grandfatherly man, a retired state fire marshall and disabled veteran, that finding an old house was "near impossible." This was more helpful than I could have imagined. It was almost a relief. Again, he pressed my hand in a polite handshake.

I stepped back into the piercing blue sunlight and walked carefully down the grassy hill to my car. I actually envied his ability to let go. I started to wonder what was wrong with me. Why did I care about these old houses? Was there really any attachment to begin with? Or was the prospect of motherhood messing with my head? My lost mom, lost babies, lost cities all merging into one impossibly devastating hormonal sludge? Why couldn't I be more like Cole and the firemen—above nostalgia? Knowing that buildings don't last, they can't last. You just make a new home in a new place and call it progress.

Behind me came the dull chime of a chain flapping against a flagpole. Then a descending jet blotted out the sound. I sat in my sun-warmed car for a few minutes facing the fire station, a low, cinder block bunker on a busy commercial thoroughfare. Cole spent decades moving through this building—working, eating, sleeping. The firehouse, with its unchanging rhythms and boyish energy. It was the place where he wanted to meet; the place where he felt at home.

A FEW DAYS LATER, I drove down to Riverdale to see Cole's "development" on East Fayetteville Drive. The highway wound around the base of the Fifth Runway. Here was the subject of one of Cole's few sentimental observations. "I look out where the planes are landing and think, that's where I used to live," he said.

High on trapezoidal hills, the cruising fins of aircraft seem to circulate around a still, isolated core.

From the airport, the drive stretched southward through heavily wooded areas dotted with the scars of old houses and a number of new residential subdivisions. It was a swath of Clayton County that was completely unfamiliar to me. I recognized the name of a high school that I knew only as a "black" high school. So this was North Clayton. How had I never ventured here before? Again, I sensed the pattern of a flight path neighborhood as a kind of modern ghetto, racially segregated and physically cut off.

I was surprised to see that East Fayetteville Drive, once I found it, still felt semi-rural. The short road dead-ended into a yellow pasture. No livestock was present, but a spray-painted plank hammered to a fencepost said: "Please don't feed the horses."

And the duplexes—two houses welded together with a porch— had held up well. They resembled long brick ranches with a driveway on each end. Not only were they all occupied, they looked tidy, comfortable. The whole neighborhood did. A basketball goal stood halfway down the block and I spotted a tire swing in a tree. Like the former residents of Mountain View, scattered across the southside, the houses had new lives. If these tiny, faceless brick boxes had value, surely my old house could be successfully transplanted too. Perhaps it was out on some country road, looking prim and solid, like it had been there all along.

As a thin woman with four children walked past my parked car, I wondered if they knew about the transient past of their homes. Why would they? These duplexes had been standing twice as long as the original houses. They were older than I. The airplanes landing to the north drew small lines behind the bare trees. The sound of an occasional surge reached this place like distant ocean waves carried on the breeze.

Former site of Gilbert Gardens, a housing project off Poole Creek Road, 2016.

SEVENTEEN

PLUNKYTOWN TO

POOLE CREEK

I met Tara Taylor while touring daycare facilities in East Point. Shopping for childcare brought back memories of house hunting. I felt hopeful yet vulnerable, always one step behind on the jargon and paperwork. The facility was only a small part of the decision. The people, the location, even the smell of the place combined to start me dreaming involuntarily of our life in that particular church basement, those linoleum tiled hallways, this craggy parking lot. I wanted to fall in love with a place; to get married. I didn't know if my educational philosophy was leaning towards Bible-based curriculum, Montessori, or prep school prep. My kid wasn't even born yet, but suddenly I had to know these things. As I headed into parenthood, the decision about daycare loomed large as one of the pillars of our future.

I made appointments at three different preschools near our house. One was housed in the Sunday school wing of College Park First Methodist, a rambling brick institution that had expanded over time to accommodate a congregation that had since vanished. I thought about how the population of College Park was halved by airport acquisitions. I thought of the dwindling congregation at my home church, where the youngest members were grey-haired grandparents, like my parents. As a lapsed Methodist, something about paying to use surplus church space made me feel vaguely depressed and guilty.

The other two preschools were located in a turn-of-the-century industrial complex that had been adapted as lofts, offices and clinics, a conversion that made me feel more optimistic.

All three daycare places were sunny and clean, bursting with colorful toys and happy noise, shin-height tables and mini-toilets. All three cost around a thousand bucks per month, a price tag that made me lightheaded, but was still cheaper than what my friends claimed they were paying in better parts of town. Though the children in these facilities represented a delightful spectrum of chubby pink and brown faces, I observed that all three schools were staffed almost exclusively by black and Hispanic women.

Ms. Tara was one of the baby-whisperers working in the "nido," or the nest, at the Montessori school. My first impression of the place was that everything in the room was elf-sized and low to the ground. Next, I noticed that the room was unusually calm. The other nurseries I had visited were filled with crying babies wedged in high chairs, cribs, and Bumbo seats, and I assumed the noise level was normal. Here, there was no crying.

Ms. Tara was seated on a cushion on the floor, jiggling one baby in a bouncy chair while another infant snoozed against her chest. She was wearing dark skinny jeans and a trendy striped blouse, hair arranged in a sleek bob, without a trace of baby spit up or disarray. All around me, babies shuffled, swiped at toys and slept, but none cried. I wanted to take notes.

I settled on a floor cushion for my little interview, which was mostly me marveling at the quiet rhythm of the room, occasionally asking about bottles and diapers and naps. As we chatted, it didn't take long for Tara and me to learn the things we had in common. She had her first son at twenty-one, putting her a decade ahead of me in maternal wisdom. We were both from the southside—I graduated from Forest

Park High in '96, she was class of '98 at Tri-Cities. As we zeroed in on our home turf, we discovered another connection. Tara remembered Mountain View, and even better, she knew about its black counterpart, Plunkett Town.

"I've never been there, but my pastor is always telling stories about Plunkytown," she said.

Here in the middle of my childcare investigation, I lit up.

"You know about that place?" I said. "There's nothing on the Internet about Plunkett Town. I can't find anything."

"I'll tell you right now, it's Plunkytown," she said, laughing. "That's your problem."

One's pastor and church are a personal subject, but we were already talking about breastfeeding and healing from childbirth, so I asked Tara to introduce me to this Plunkett Town native. When she told me the name of her church—Valley View Church of God in Christ—she said it with this proud smile, like the place was legendary and I should know about it already.

"He can tell you about Plunkytown or he'll find someone. There's about a dozen of them old folks that are always talking about it."

VALLEY VIEW CHURCH OF GOD in Christ was located in a Southeast Atlanta neighborhood five miles north of the former Plunkett Town. This was quasi-familiar territory for me, near the intersection of roads I had driven a thousand times without knowing or wondering much about the communities hidden in between. I had never ventured off the main road, past the pawnshops and tire stacks at Hub Cap Daddy. There was no reason for me, a white person, to go there.

I realized this as I exited Moreland Avenue and zig-zagged through a patch of low brick homes that resembled the early 1960s housing stock in Forest Park where I grew up. It was Friday afternoon and there were no other cars or people around. A lawnmower stood in a driveway. Pinwheels turned in a flowerbed ringed by whitewashed tires. I followed a series of streets named for Confederates: Rebel Forest Drive, Stonewall, O'Hara. I passed, in order, signs for Nathan, Bedford, and Forrest Drives.

I took Locust Lane until it ended abruptly at a row of concrete jersey barriers. Valley View Church, as its name suggested, stood there at the top of a hill overlooking a meadow of wildflowers. Expecting simply to locate the church and maybe take some photos, I was surprised to find Pastor Gary Cooper at the bottom of the driveway, chatting with the postman by the mailbox. He seemed happy to see me.

"You're the one that called about Plunkytown," he said. "Sister Tara's friend? Come inside, I have something for you."

He bounded up the hill, outpacing me quickly. He was tall and wiry, wearing a blue Adidas tracksuit, and surprisingly fit for a pastor in his late sixties. Maybe he was much younger, I thought. What did I know about any of this?

He disappeared into the back door of the sanctuary, looking for whatever it was he wanted to give me. I waited outside for a moment, studying the church. The sanctuary was a large brick trapezoid with no steeple. A formal stairway flanked by neatly-squared shrubs led to the white double doors at the entrance. Behind that was a two-story white cinder block building, probably a Sunday school wing. A scalloped aluminum awning over the door was its only defining adornment.

The church was aging, but tidy and loved. I pictured Pastor Gary spending his mornings here on a riding lawnmower, as Christ loved the church. On a hazy spring day when pollen dusted every surface like snow, Pastor Gary's gunmetal SUV was pristine.

Where did he go? I stepped into the dim sanctuary. This had to be my first time inside a black church, and not only that, my first time inside a Church of God in Christ, which is a Pentecostal denomination. Though they dotted every corner of Atlanta's southside, I had never visited one before and didn't know what to expect.

My eyes adjusted to the amber light streaming through the patterned glass windows. I saw two rows of dark wooden pews and a long central aisle leading up to a wood-paneled altar and baptismal font. A series of modest mid-century pendant lamps lined the aisle. Symmetrical silk flower arrangements by the pulpit. Small stacks of Bibles, tracts, and brass offering plates on a table by the door. It looked like any Protestant sanctuary from my childhood.

Pastor Cooper returned and presented me with a printed program from their 2002 homecoming service. We stepped back outside into the light to flip through the booklet together. It was sixty pages of Bible verses, blurry black and white photos, and tributes to congregants who had joined the saints. Exactly the kind of document I used to compile every day at Bellamy Printing.

The book included a brief biography of his father, Bishop John Cooper, the founder of Valley View. He and his wife, Mother Grace Cooper, started a music ministry in a revival tent in Plunkett Town in 1958. He named it the Hapeville Church of God in Christ and built a church on a piece of land that his brother sold him for $500. Pastor Gary told me the old folks called the area "Mudline," because the streets were unpaved and often slick with mud. He remembered pausing during sermons and testimonials while airplanes flew overhead, but that the music continued right through the noise.

In 1971, Bishop Cooper purchased their current building from a white Baptist congregation. Here, the Valley View Church continued to grow, along with Bishop Cooper's influence, producing pastors and planting at least eight other churches, broadcasting sermons on the radio and gospel music on local television. Famed for its music program, Valley View revivals were known to last until the wee hours of the morning, with the post-sermon altar call lasting a few hours each night.

"Do you think a lot of people from Plunkett Town ended up around here?" I asked.

He shrugged, as though it was impossible to estimate.

"They just scattered, went all over." Suddenly, he brightened. "You know the Pace Sisters?"

I had to admit that I had never heard of them.

"Gospel singers. Must be about nine of them. The whole family grew up with us in Plunkytown and here at Valley View. You should ask them about it."

As we walked down the hill to my car, I noticed that the meadow across the street was encircled by a tall fence topped with barbed wire. Another barricaded road, mysteriously fortified, trailed off behind the fence.

"So what is this valley?" I asked. "Why is the church called Valley View?"

"That was just the name. It used to be Valley View Baptist and my father changed it to Valley View Church of God in Christ."

"But what used to be over there?" I pointed to the grassy field.

"That used to be the projects. Leila Valley Apartments. They tore it down around 2008."

He pronounced it *Leela*. Again, a place that clearly held some notoriety, though I had never heard of it. The layers of my cultural illiteracy were humbling. I tried to imagine that field being home to hundreds of people, the site of a small city for who knows how long. A truncated sidewalk was the only remaining vestige of the apartments. I asked Pastor Gary if people missed Leila Valley. Another dumb question.

"I don't really miss it because of all the crime. Gunshots, broken glass." He shuddered. For a preacher, he was actually a man of few words. "No. It's better now."

I let it lie. Something to research later, along with the Pace Sisters.

As I left, Pastor Gary shook my hand and told me to say hello to Sister Tara and tell her he missed her on Sundays. He joked that he was going to come after her.

I know from years of backsliding what it means when someone says, "We missed you on Sunday." It means that your lack of church attendance has been noted. It's as much a coded reprimand as "bless your heart."

I drove home on back roads, through black neighborhoods that I had avoided for my entire life. The road passed from spotty residential areas to light industrial with no warning, no transition. I passed more churches than gas stations, libraries, schools, or restaurants. Churches on every corner, like sentinels: The Greater Epheseus Missionary Baptist Church, Message of Truth Ministries, New Life Tabernacle of Faith Church of God in Christ, United House of Prayer for All People, and the Maranatha Seventh Day Adventist Church. There hardly seemed to be enough houses to fill the pews. I drove from Valley View to the warehouses where Plunkett Town used to be, on to Hapeville, where airplanes pounded down in twos and threes.

Later on, reading the Valley View homecoming booklet, I pieced together more of the church history. The Annual Family and Friends Day of 2002 was a turning point for Valley View and possibly a high-water mark for church attendance. Bishop John Cooper, Pastor Gary's father and the church founder, had just passed away, leaving his son with the task of mobilizing a church whose membership was aging and moving out of the area. Pastor Gary, who so lovingly maintained the church building, no longer lived in Southeast Atlanta but twenty miles to the east in middle-class suburb called Stone Mountain. Tara and her family now lived in rural Fairburn, twenty miles to the south. From Plunkett Town to Southeast Atlanta to the suburbs, the black community had its own series of migrations. The pattern gave me a familiar heartburn.

What was left was a cavernous church on a dead end road by a vacant lot where even the projects had been cleared.

How could I learn more about Plunkett Town and the African-American neighborhoods that were bought out around the same time as Mountain View? Both the black and white communities were physically erased, the streets renamed, and there was nothing on the Internet to guide my research. The only way to get information was to talk to people who remembered the area, and that was not easy. As with Mountain View, a lingering hush remained over these places, and people seemed cautious and uncertain about what had happened there.

White folks called it Plunkett Town, black folks remembered it as something that rhymes with Funkytown. Even the spelling of the place was unclear. Originally established in the late 1930s as a settlement for blacks, Plunkett Town was considered a slum area, cut off from such city services as paved roads, sanitation services, and in some cases, plumbing and electricity. Photos of Plunkett Town from the late 1970s show the original clapboard structures propped up and leaning, prone to fires and collapse.

The more I inquired about Plunkett Town, the more I heard references to "Poole Creek," another place I had never heard of. What little evidence I could find of Poole Creek made it seem mythical, a world that had grown in legend since disappearing from the landscape. For example, the gospel group The Anointed Pace Sisters, founding members of Pastor Cooper's church in Plunkett Town, sang about the place. I found a 1993 recording of a performance of "Back to Poole Creek" on YouTube.

As the grainy video opened, singer LaShun Pace, wearing a long sequined jacket, stood at the front of a crowded church sanctuary. Her mother, a smaller woman in purple, swayed by her side. The altar was lined with Easter lilies, the pews packed with congregants fluttering paper fans.

"Y'all know how God would name a certain place in the Bible?" she began, smiling as if she was among friends. "This place shall be named Poole Creek."

Approving cheers came from the congregation. I couldn't believe my luck.

"In Poole Creek you came to know God in a very real way. There was a lot of hard times in Poole Creek. You shed many tears in Poole Creek."

She half sang, half preached in a powerful soprano voice, each line punctuated by a flourish from the organist. This is what's called in the Pentecostal tradition the "sermonic hymn," a showstopper that gets the entire congregation energized before the sermon.

"But not only was Poole Creek a place of tears and sorrow, but God took Poole Creek and turned it into a river of joy. And he turned it into a sea of love."

LaShun beckoned to her sisters and brother to join her onstage.

"He took the sea of love and turned it into an ocean of life. Who was it that brought you through all those years?"

Mother Betty Ann Pace stepped forward to lead the chorus, eyes closed. When she let loose the first sustained notes, "When I look out around me I see what the Lord has done for me," my arms broke out in goosebumps. Aretha Franklin was my only frame of reference. The Pace siblings gathered around their mother and two standing microphones, turning their backs to the audience and the cameras. At this point, the choir and most of the congregation were on their feet.

Watching the eleven-minute video, I realized that this was the first time music had ever seeped into my research. It gave me chills to hear Poole Creek described as a site of biblical tribulation. I didn't have to ask what the place meant to LaShun Pace, or how she felt about its demise. She was singing the story in all its complexity, turning tears shed into a river of joy. By the time Father Pace took the mic, people were leaping and dancing in the aisles and I was wiping away tears. They all had their own version of Poole Creek.

I recognized this combination of pride and sadness about being from the southside, from a place in decline, irretrievable. But where was Poole Creek exactly? And what happened to it?

You don't have to go far back to find maps that show Poole Creek Road in Southeast Atlanta. The road started at Plunkett Town, near Old Dixie Highway, and ended at Jonesboro Road near its namesake waterway. Today, the road is named Southside Industrial Parkway, a 1.75-mile curve through a dismal landscape of warehouses and overgrown, vacant land, with no creek in sight. This is a recurring scene on all sides of the airport, and as I drove the wide and pot-holed parkway, I looked for remaining traces of a neighborhood. Did the airport wipe out Poole Creek?

The *Noise Land Reuse Plan* had a whole section on Poole Creek, confirming that the airport acquired approximately 455 homes on Poole Creek Road in the early 1980s using a combination of federal community development block grants and Airport Improvement Program funds. I also located Gilbert Gardens, a 220-unit public housing project near Poole Creek Road. It was built under the flight path, and demolished in 2005. Today, about half of the land has been redeveloped for light industrial uses, warehouses, and offices. The other lots sit empty and haunted, crumbling driveways and fences still marking the entrance to old homes.

Based on the Pace Sisters' song and these airport records, it appeared that Poole Creek had been a poor black neighborhood just over the county line and just inside the worst noise contour. On one side was Plunkett Town, a dilapidated 1930s settlement for blacks, and on the other was Gilbert Gardens, a housing project just as segregated and dilapidated by the 1980s.

But there was more; Poole Creek Road cut across a white neighborhood too. Deep in the online message boards about Gilbert Gardens a strange line jumped out at me: "I can tell by your feet that you come from Poole Creek."

You don't have to know about Poole Creek to understand it's an insult, a playground taunt. I asked Ms. Tara if she had any idea what it meant. She laughed at me. She'd heard kids chanting it at Vacation Bible School just last summer.

"It means you need a pedicure," she told me. "It means you look broke."

Imagine my surprise when I started to share this little artifact with my dad and he finished the rhyme for me. He remembered the line from childhood and said it had a similar meaning for white kids in Forest Park in the 1950s. It was a way of calling someone poor or low class. It was an insult lobbed at the kids from Blair Village. But he couldn't explain clearly what Blair Village was, or where, exactly.

So I went back to my two best sources, Facebook reunion groups and Franklin Garrett's massive, three-volume history *Atlanta and Environs*. He mentions Blair Village in a section about one of Atlanta's earliest settlers, Adam Poole.

"A new low-rental apartment development, known as Blair Village, now occupies the site of the Poole settlement. One of the principal streets in the Village retains the Poole name as Poole Creek Drive, while the Poole family cemetery was carefully built around and the site not destroyed."

I joined a lively Facebook group called "Blair Village Survivors," where I became member number 359. All of us, judging by the profile pics, were white. The group's collective photos and memories of Blair Village conjure a place that seems like a world unto itself. Commenters were mostly there to share childhood memories of "a more innocent time"—late summer nights skateboarding down Wascanna Road, floating in the pool, cookouts in the courtyards, chasing girls at the drive-in theater. The apartments themselves were not as beloved as the life that took place in the courtyards, the woods, the basketball court, and the creek. In photos of prom dates and snowball fights, the apartments line up in the background, solid, square and plain.

Historic aerial photos showed a street pattern of sweeping loops off Poole Creek Road, dotted by low brick cottages clustered around a courtyard—a kind of low-budget, low-density garden style configuration. At about 200 acres, Blair Village was almost as big as the city of Mountain View, and with 300 buildings, the development likely rivaled its population too.

Not everyone remembers Blair Village as the good old days. Some commenters were candid about crime and traumatic memories. One commenter said the Village should be called "hell on earth" and that he felt safer when they moved to Capitol Homes, a notorious public housing project.

So was Blair Village "the projects"? Its uniformity in design, almost military in its precision, coupled with Garrett's description as a "low rental" development, caused me to wonder. Atlanta pioneered public housing in the late '30s with Techwood Homes, an all-white housing project that replaced a black slum known as Techwood Flats. Was Blair Village a white housing project?

This led me to an even bigger question: what exactly are "the projects" anyways? And why does it matter what we call them? Gilbert Gardens, built right next door to Blair Village in 1970, was developed, owned and maintained by the Atlanta Housing Authority using federal funds. It was by definition "the projects," and it became, over time, exclusively inhabited by African-American families and infamous for drugs and crime. Few people can explain the technical definition of affordable or public housing, but the meaning of "the projects" has grown to include any standardized housing that isolates and concentrates crime and poverty.

When Blair Village opened in 1951 it was the largest apartment complex in the city, bigger than Techwood Homes, Carver Homes, or any multi-family development, public or private during the post-war housing boom in Atlanta. Nearby, Ford's Hapeville assembly plant and GM's Lakewood assembly plant provided steady blue-collar jobs to returning WWII vets, creating demand for housing. The vast majority of apartments built in Georgia from late 1940s to early '50s were financed and underwritten by the U.S. Federal Housing Authority (FHA). Federal funds subsidized low-income white housing, but it wasn't called "the projects" and it didn't carry the stigma.

I found a startling 1963 map of Atlanta's "Negro Residential Areas" that highlighted one side of Poole Creek as a "Negro Area-1962," with the other side marked "Transitional 1968." Blair Village was white, but after the Civil Rights Act of 1964, it was illegal to enforce such racial segregation. By 1968, the swimming pool at Blair Village was filled in with dirt and the complex was losing residents. It would not survive the transition to desegregation.

So what happened to Blair Village? It appears that rather than integrate with the poor black community next door, the owners allowed the complex to deteriorate as residents moved out. I found the 1979

Neighborhood Plan for NPU-Z, the "neighborhood planning unit," which included distinct boundaries for Plunkett Town, Poole Creek, Gilbert Gardens, and Blair Village. The plan, a four-page pamphlet really, recommended the demolition of Blair Village, calling it "not fit for human habitation."

"While most of the NPU's housing is in good condition, two areas are showing signs of major deterioration: Blair Village and Plunkett Town. Blair Village, a 1,100 unit publicly-subsidized housing complex, is approximately 68 percent vacant. Most of the units are deteriorated, and are being boarded up as they are vacated."

The plan also recommends that residents in the area be relocated because of excessive noise from the airport, and that the property be converted to industrial uses. Blair Village was demolished by 1981, at the same time 455 houses next door on Poole Creek Road were acquired by the airport. The money came from different sources, but the effect—slum clearance—was the same. Blair Village, home to thousands for thirty years, was completely wiped out and replaced by warehouses.

Which came first, the slums or the airport? It's impossible to separate the twin forces of airport expansion and white flight, both somewhat triggered by policy and plans of 1964. Either way, Blair Village and Plunkett Town were bad parts of town that only got worse as airport noise increased. Blair Village survivors are generally uncertain about what happened to the place. They debate on Facebook—did the airport buy it or the city? Just as in Mountain View, the displaced see its erasure with resignation and suspicion, or as a kind of cleansing, or just part of the passage of time.

When whites fled to Clayton County and the outer suburbs, they turned their backs on the City of Atlanta and its integrated swimming pools, streetcars, and housing projects. At that time there were no housing projects in Clayton County. For a short period, the county line acted as a color line, an invisible boundary as stark as the noise contours.

The black communities near the airport had a flight path too, but it led into Southeast Atlanta where there were new public housing projects and affordable homes vacated by white flight. At some point in the late 1960s, the white congregation of Valley View Baptist stood watching the Leila Valley Apartments under construction across the street and decided to place a For Sale sign on their door.

Despite the excessive noise from the airport, it took decades for the airport to buy out Gilbert Gardens, a $7 million transaction in 2004 between the Atlanta Housing Authority and another powerful city agency, the Department of Aviation. The timing suggests that Gilbert Gardens was shut down not because of noise but as part of the Atlanta Housing Authority's new agenda to eradicate its traditional, large-scale housing projects. Starting with Techwood Homes during the 1996 Olympics, the housing authority began demolishing these "warehouses for the poor" and replacing them with "mixed-income communities" funded by public-private partnerships. By 2009, Atlanta became the first major American city to demolish all of its "projects."

In the case of Gilbert Gardens and Leila Valley, however, the projects were never replaced or rebuilt. The grassy meadow at Leila Valley belies a gaping hole in Atlanta's psycho-geography. Gilbert Gardens is a ghost town. The roads remain, crumbling and weedy. Young pines thread the tilted iron fence. Combined with the former neighborhood along Poole Creek Road, sixty acres of noise land sit undisturbed. I saw "DOA" spray-painted on several jersey barriers before I realized it meant Department of Aviation, not "dead on arrival."

One block over, on the other side of the invisible 75-decibel noise contour, a ring of low brick houses and an elementary school remain on Blair Villa Drive. No fewer than three small white steeples appear through the trees: Solomon Temple Baptist, Little Mount Gilead, and the Divine House of Praise. Each church is built from the same brick as the houses.

My mom, pregnant in Mountain View, 1978.

EIGHTEEN

NESTING

One month until my due date and my husband was rewir-
ing the house. He felt confident enough with *The Creative
Homeowner's Ultimate Guide to Wiring* and YouTube
instructional videos and the advice of a few handy friends to attempt
the work of a licensed electrician. The oversized breaker box in our
hallway sat exposed for weeks where he removed the door by the
hinges.

I loved his fearless do-it-yourself approach, but the whole project
worried me. We should have, at least, acquired permits for this work.
I wouldn't allow myself to think about the consequences of wiring
mistakes. "A hundred twenty volts won't kill anyone!" Jason vowed,
laughing. He had drawn all these color-coded wiring diagrams and
repeatedly explained his plans. Whatever he's doing, I told myself, it
can't be any worse than the outdated and frayed wiring that already
powered our house.

Jason was replacing the original, armored cable that snaked
through the walls with coils of modern, yellow, rubber-sheathed wire.
While he had already painstakingly painted every corner of every
room, including all the white gloss trim and window sills, this rewir-
ing struck me as his most intimate home improvement to date. No

one could see the work he was doing, but we felt it. He showed me the melted, rusty receptacles he'd wrenched out of the walls. A bundle of ropy, metal wire on the front porch waited to be recycled. It was as though Jason had touched the insides of the walls now and claimed them. With each shiny new outlet, in fact, he shoved sunshine through the dark and decaying channels of our house.

While I was snooping around the airport, chatting with firemen, house movers, and southside veterans, my husband was pulling wire. We had our own ways of nesting.

When I came home, he would emerge from the basement crawlspace wearing a dingy dust mask and head lamp, with bits of insulation clinging in his hair. He would eagerly start to tell me about the latest wiring mystery solved. I just wanted to know when the work would be done.

At first, it was hard for me to go on these expeditions without him. With a tall, easygoing conversationalist like Jason at my side, it was easy to get strangers talking. His Forest Park accent opened doors the same way my maiden name did. Together, we looked more like a curious young couple and less like trespassers. Alone, I looked like a reporter and a pregnant one at that. There I was, silently wobbling through these airport dead zones on a perfectly lovely Saturday morning. Many places just weren't safe enough to visit alone. The tire-littered jungles of Mountain View beckoned from the roadside, but I stayed in my car. No telling who or what was growing back there. But he wasn't just a bodyguard; I needed Jason there to help me make sense of things, to help me remember the details.

We had known about the shoddy wiring since we bought the house six years before. During our first week as homeowners we hired an electrician, a friend of my father, to install a 220-volt outlet in the basement for the dryer. He took one look overhead at the tangle of old and new wires and judged it "some real Mickey Mouse shit." I had no idea what he meant, but the way he said it, I knew it couldn't be good. Over the years, we discovered other dire code

violations that should've been revealed in the initial house inspection. The overloaded breaker box. Mystery outlets that carried half
a charge. Nothing grounded. Once, during an electrical storm, Jason
watched a blue ball of light coalesce a few inches in front of a floor
outlet, expand, and then fizzle in a burst of static electricity. Good
thing the house hadn't burned down.

So we always knew our house needed to be completely rewired.
But it became a sudden priority when I started "showing." I had
heard stories of irrational, urgent nesting projects in the months leading up to childbirth. Pregnant women cleaning out their closets in
the wee hours of the morning. Fathers-to-be organizing the medicine
cabinet or alphabetizing bookshelves. Jason's project, though not
exactly irrational, was an ambitious undertaking.

And it wasn't just the wiring. With his typical hyperfocus magnified by fatherhood, each wire led to new projects. Light fixtures and
ceiling fans that we'd never really liked—why not replace them now?
And where an old light fixture left a hole by the front door, why not
repair the vinyl siding? All the siding, in fact, could use a good pressure washing. While crawling around in the basement, he was com-
pelled to investigate the leaking tub drain. He determined that now
was also the time to replace all the plastic sheeting in the crawlspace.
This led to an all-day basement clean-out session, complete with new
overhead bike hooks. Jason spent hours repairing chipped plaster
around the extracted outlets—spackling, scraping, and repainting.
He hunted down new fixtures and switches and wire-pulling devices.
He recruited friends to devote their weekends to the cause. In the
space of a few months, he tackled household upgrades that we had
been putting off for years.

At the same time, I was losing the ability to bend over and tie my
shoes or lift a laundry basket. I stood by approvingly and tried not to
worry about the projects spawning projects. I swept up plaster dust,
wire casings, and rusted junction boxes. Really, we just needed to
assemble the crib.

"I hear babies really appreciate GFI outlets," I joked with my sister.

"He's nesting more than you are," she replied, not really kidding. I started to protest this sisterly jab, but what did she know? It may not look all that maternal, but what about all my hours in the deed office, untangling the details of our old houses? All my decoding of aerial maps of the runways, estimating flight vectors and calculating how many years we might have here? Sure, I hadn't organized the nursery yet, but I had tracked down and revisited South West Street, Barnett Road, and Phillips Drive—all the sacred grounds of our childhood— until they no longer held any power over me. I even finished *Gone With the Wind*, out of all the parenting books on my nightstand. It was a thousand pages long.

My parents—all three of them—visited regularly to check on our progress with the wiring and the nursery. I overheard Jason telling my father about his last Saturday in the crawlspace. He had used a garden shovel to scrape under the cast-iron pipe that connected our plumbing to the city sewer line. He created a trench just deep enough so he could shimmy under it and feed a wire up to the front of the house. He had a brief moment of claustrophobia as he struggled to drill a hole for the wire with the weight of those pipes across his chest.

"I thought, if for any reason I needed to get out of here real fast, I am going to freak out."

True, this was not a comforting anecdote for a pregnant wife to hear. Even so, I have learned it is good to tune in when the men bring out their "work stories." My dad, brother, and grandfathers have told Jason tales of blue-collar pranks, off-color injuries, job site skirmishes, near-death experiences, and other such manly war stories that they would never otherwise share with me. Once they got going, there were always some repeats and some surprises.

"After we moved out of the house on South West Street, I did something similar," Dad said. "Your mother asked me to help her move her kiln from the porch and I said I'd do it."

What? Mom dumped him, broke his heart, and then asked him to help move the kiln? A half-ton piece of equipment, hardwired to the house? And he did it?

"So I flipped the breaker and crawled down in the basement with a pair of loppers to cut the wire," he said. "I was on my back, just about to cut it when I had second thoughts. I lay there wondering, 'Did I flip the right switch?' I thought and thought about it, but I couldn't be sure."

Eventually, my father crawled back out of the basement and discovered that he had not disconnected the right breaker, and he had been moments away from electrocution.

"No one knew I was under there. They wouldn't have found me until I started to stink." They laughed.

Or until they picked up the house and rolled it away. I filed away this story as more warped evidence that Mom and Dad once shared a house and a pottery kiln.

Whenever Jason told me a story from his childhood, like the time he burned the skin off his toes stomping out a secret "experiment" that caught fire, or when his sister Cindy spray-painted the initials "CP" on every tree in the backyard, or when the next-door neighbor got struck by lightning, or the time David Turner got the breath knocked out of him after he failed to clear the creek on his bike, despite the plywood ramps they had constructed for the event, and they tried reviving him with a water hose, my first question is always, "Now, how old were you when this happened?"

Jason is never quite sure of his age, because he spent his whole childhood in one place—the house on Karla Circle in Conley. He claims the years bleed together in his memory. He will then perform a little equation like, "It was after Matt got his Beetle but before Mom died, so that would be '88, '89." Or, "That was the year we got matching bikes for Christmas and right after that, Van busted his spleen on his handlebars, so I was probably eleven."

It's not that he's forgetful. Jason's stories render detail as if he's describing a video he's edited, or a painting he's studied. It's just that houses define one's sense of a personal timeline, and his lasted his whole life.

Unlike my lost houses, the Palmer residence was still standing, a small brick ranch with a dirt yard directly in the flight path.

Jason remembered that there were always a half dozen kids around to play with. The way he talked, whole tribes of boys roamed the streets unsupervised, building skate ramps, practicing breakdance moves, and starting fires. The houses were too small to contain them.

Conley was an unincorporated community north of Forest Park, a hub for commercial trucking directly under the flight path of Hartsfield-Jackson's north runways. And though the airport purchased air rights in the 1980s, it did little to stop the freefall of property values. The flight path was like an invisible freeway over the neighborhood. For homeowners, it meant thousands of dollars vanished into thin air.

Jason's father owned 4556 Karla Circle from the time it was built up until a couple years ago. He was preparing to sell it when vandals gutted the house for scrap metal. They ripped into the walls for the pipes and copper wiring, raided the basement, attic, and garage. They even extracted the doorknobs. Since then, my father-in-law has given up on the property. He turned the keys over to the bank.

Many times we have driven down Karla Circle to pay our respects. Every crevice was nostalgic for Jason, but to me, the house was small and somber. It's so weak and foreign it almost makes me grateful that I can't revisit my old houses. The quest to find them was supposed to end with a scene where I walk up the oddly familiar steps and knock on the front door. I was supposed to have a polite confrontation with the new residents and their inappropriate belongings. Or better yet, I'm supposed to take my son by the hand to show him these places, explaining where I used to watch Gramma make pottery, or where my bed overlooked the backyard, or we bashed pecans on the back stoop.

If my old houses were moved, if they are sitting on new foundations, facing east instead of west, or north instead of south, somewhere far away from the airport, I have not found them. There is no preparing for parenthood; only research as a form of prayer and manic speculation.

There's the powerful sense that the hedges and bricks are colorless and small, that it might be better if they disappeared.

NINETEEN

AEROTROPOLIS
ATLANTA

A barn-shaped outpost on the east edge of the Atlanta airport, Blanchard's Bakery was one of the few businesses in Mountain View to survive the last thirty-something years of runway expansion. The rest of the neighborhood packed up and moved south, but Blanchard's remained on Old Dixie Highway, serving up sausage biscuits and birthday cakes to Delta ground crews and other airport employees.

It was almost 6:00 PM and the small shop was filled with amber sunlight when I slipped in the door. An oscillating fan behind the cash register stirred up the smell of sugar while a young woman with bleached blonde hair served the last customer of the day. An unseen radio back in the kitchen delivered the traffic report.

I found myself instantly craving doughnuts, the old-fashioned variety, oblong and glazed. I must have come here for doughnuts as a child. All I remember is the happy anticipation of just driving by Blanchard's Bakery, knowing there were countless cupcakes lined up inside. This was the same spot where I met the Stovalls for our tour of Mountain View.

The place hadn't changed much since I was a kid. Rotating in a display case, there was a fake wedding cake that might have been iced in the '80s. The young woman behind the counter passed a white paper bag to her customer and then turned to me. Her frosty bangs and pink cheeks like white pastry bags full of icing—voluptuous and sweet. I leaned over the glass display case lined with oversized cookies and brightly-colored petit-fours and instead of ordering one, I asked what she thought about the big redevelopment project across the street. Did she know what was happening at the old Ford assembly plant?

When I heard the term "Aerotropolis" applied to Hapeville, I was cautiously intrigued. Despite sounding like marketing spin, it was the first time I could remember anyone proposing something constructive on the fringe of the airport. Out of this industrial wasteland, an "airport city" would be born. Never mind the city that was there in the first place. I went to Blanchard's curious about the disconnect between this new vision and the old remnants of Mountain View.

"All I know is they're tearing down the plant," she said. She glanced at the clock and smiled helplessly. "Now the owner, she's not here, but she could tell you all about it."

I placed two color prints on the countertop. They showed a series of aerial plans and architectural renderings from the developers' websites.

"Have you seen what they're proposing?"

She gazed over the drawings. The 128-acre site of the old Hapeville Ford plant, currently a massive demolition zone, would eventually be filled in with shops and restaurants, a hotel and sports club, corporate offices, and a "data center campus," all lined with puffy little trees. Because of the decibel level of the location, the FAA restricted residential development throughout the site. The lower half of the property sat so close to the airport's northernmost runways, it's been designated as a "Runway Object Free" zone, which prohibits all development. Half of Aerotropolis Atlanta would be a parking lot.

These restrictions pushed residential development next door, where the Asbury Park "urban village" fits two thousand housing units on thirty-three acres. This proposed "city within a city" includes luxury apartments, faux-historic townhouses, condos and lofts, complete with striped awnings, sidewalk cafes, and parks. When completed, it would double the number of households in Hapeville.

"It's called an Aerotropolis," I said. "Like, an airport city."

"That's wild," she murmured, shaking her head. "I just thought the airport bought it."

Not the airport, but a host of eager developers, including Jacoby Development, the same group behind Atlantic Station, a case study for successful brownfield redevelopment in Atlanta. Located on the former site of Atlantic Steel, their 2005 development transformed a massive industrial site into a mixed-use district. Atlantic Station was, by all commercial measures, a triumph. But it felt like a mall, not a city.

"It's gonna be too crowded," she said, after a moment. "I mean. For Hapeville?" She took a closer look at one sheet and then handed it back to me.

We made small talk while she packed a half dozen peanut butter cookies for me and a few chocolate chip for Jason. Just like my family, she was from here but migrated south, towards rural Thomaston, which is almost sixty miles away. Also like my family, she continued to commute to Atlanta daily for work.

"We're thinking about moving back up this way," she said. "I work here and my husband drives a truck, and with gas prices..."

"Maybe you can move to one of those townhouses they're building?" I said.

She gave me a blank look, like I'd said something clever in French. "That's $6.42, please."

It was past closing time now, and a box truck sat idling in the parking lot, waiting for her. Late afternoon sun caught the sugary smudges on the glass door. She will be gone soon, I thought. As I thanked her, I heard my own dripping Southern accent.

LOOKING AT THE RENDERINGS for the planned, multibillion-dollar, mixed-used development intended to replace the old Ford plant, I was struck by the genuine, cash-fueled ambition of the project. If even half of the developers' proposal came to fruition, Hapeville would transition from a sleepy Southern town to "Aerotropolis Atlanta."

Aerotropolis. I took a sliver of satisfaction learning the name for this place.

Author John T. Kasarda coined the term in his 2012 book *Aerotropolis: The Way We'll Live Next.* It labelled an urban form where cities are organized around the airport in the same way that they formed around seaports in the eighteenth century. Aerotropolis planning, or "airport urbanism," provided a hopeful vision for cities all over the world struggling with their own Mountain View complex—a ring of noise-impacted wastelands at the doorstep of their most important economic engine.

Strangely, I was coming to believe that the concept could fit this place well. Right around the corner from Blanchard's Bakery and Minuteman Printing were major UPS and FedEx hubs. From corporate headquarters to mom-and-pop locals, all the businesses were here for the airport, not for the City of Atlanta. Then there were all the conventioneers, consultants, and a whole class of portable workers who needed to flow through the airport, but not the gridlock of the city. This was the essence of the Aerotropolis concept—flipping the economic food chain so that the city is built to serve the airport, not vice versa. This idea, if implemented, could begin to address decades of disinvestment in the southside communities. The prospect of any new development bringing new jobs and services and charm was good news for any property owner around here.

But I was at a loss to justify the residential buildup that comes along with Aerotropolis Atlanta. These plans sketched in dense, residential development not in spite of, but because of the airport. There would be two thousand new homes within walking distance of the new international terminal, even closer to the runways than the former footprint of Mountain View.

Asbury Park, "a place you can call home," was the upscale residential development next to the old Ford plant. The promotional video on the developer's website included pan flute music and a sexy voiceover that makes *Asbury* rhyme with raspberry. I lost hours puzzling over the interactive site plan. The fuzzy grey areas at the edge of the rendering made it hard to situate the plans in relationship to Hapeville, or to reality. The experience was like a dream where this is your house, but it's not really your house.

The slogan for Asbury Park was *When You're Here, You're Everywhere.* I read these vague and aspirational taglines every day, and this one was a real piece of poetry. How could you be here AND everywhere? How was that different from being nowhere? Was it some nod to living practically in the airport? Where it's not clear what city, county, or state you're standing in? Or was it a reference to the simulacrum of the buildings themselves— replicas of brownstones from Chicago, New York, Boston, Philadelphia, and Georgetown. Asbury Park was perfectly at ease with its status as a made-up place, free of jurisdictions and loyalties.

Loyalties caused all the trouble. Typically, airports evolved like sewers and highways—a giant part of the civil infrastructure that everyone used, but no one loved. In fact, no one feels passionate about airports except the people who work there and the people who live nearby. And those two groups were likely to be in tension, with one gaining from the airport's growth and success, and the other losing.

In Atlanta, for a brief moment in time, those two groups were one and the same. The young facility was surrounded by neighborhoods that were home to pilots, mechanics, flight attendants and all manner of workers who made the airport tick. The pilots' homes in Hapeville were perched at the end of long, neatly landscaped driveways. In the older, blue collar neighborhoods, the houses were small, but orderly—"breeder boxes," my mom called them. There were Ford families and GM families, Eastern families and Delta families. The friendly tension between households stood in for that of a college rivalry, as most of these folks never went to college.

People used to live where they worked, and they took pride of ownership in those places. In 1968, the Ford plant, also known as

"Atlanta Assembly," reached peak employment with 4,200 workers producing hundreds of cars a day. The surrounding communities were booming, the houses contained many small worlds. These were the bedroom communities. They were the first to go.

As the airport grew, so did the distance between the employers and inhabitants, between decision-makers and the displaced. When the Ford assembly plant closed in 2006, a disproportionately small number of its 2,000 employees actually lived nearby. This was the same distance between the woman at Blanchard's Bakery and the developers reshaping her world. It's the same reason I can't find my lost houses.

Key to the success of the Aerotropolis Atlanta concept was a new and somewhat radical embrace of the airport by the people who live nearby. The Aerotropolis brand presented this formerly ignoble hunk of infrastructure as a kind of waterfront opportunity that actually adds value and a sense of place. As in, *live just minutes from your gate, minutes from takeoff.* You could be here, but on the threshold of some other city. Here and everywhere.

This shift in perception from the airport as necessary evil to the airport as cultural asset was like gentrification on a massive scale. As the city matures, like any teenager, it becomes self-conscious, it runs away, then it comes back with renewed perspective. It revises its identity again and again. A new class of Atlantans will be the ones to claim Aerotropolis Atlanta and call it home. My own discomfort with straddling these worlds amounted to a practical fear that I will not be able to afford this new city.

This first phase looked undeniably phony. The sleek new Maynard H. Jackson International Terminal glowed like a glass and steel portal to the future. But I knew it was situated across I-75 from the ruins of Mountain View. These airport embellishments appeared to me as high kitsch, simply beautifying the infrastructure without fundamentally changing anything. Like the watercolor renderings of faceless children licking ice cream cones, it seemed optimistic, but empty. Over time, certainly, this new place would start to mean something to someone. The tidy stubble of new landscaping around the new exit off I-75 would take years to grow in.

Aerotropolis Atlanta was simply reviving the concept of living where you work. But by creating a true urban mixed-use experience near the airport, the developers were inviting something unexpected: actual culture. Spaces that welcome interpretation and hacking. A "place that you can call home" would be a place where people feel a sense of authorship. Could the runways ever be our riverfront? Plane-spotting can be oddly soothing. When people claim the airport as their home, that human element is inevitable. They begin to reconcile that distance between planners and inhabitants.

The part of me that had mixed feelings about Hapeville becoming "Atlanta's newest upscale urban area" was stubbornly attached to an idea of an authentic southside. It actually felt like the South here—slow-paced, leafy with old forests and kudzu, populated by blue collar locals with deep accents. Cicadas buzzing loud enough to overcome the jet noise.

Then again, the people who arrived to work at Porsche North America, or whatever Fortune 500 companies are attracted to relocate their corporate headquarters to Aerotropolis Atlanta would be perhaps no different from the Judge's dad, Guy Benefield, who worked at the Ford plant. Or my Grandad at the Prestolite Battery plant in East Point. Only they'll be driving Porsches, not Fords.

FOR MONTHS, DEMOLITION CREWS had been taking apart the old Ford plant. I watched from the tailgate of my truck, nibbling peanut butter cookies. Bulldozers crawled all over the slumped building, pushing knots of aluminum and steel to small mountains of scrap. Twenty, or even ten years ago, this process would have been accomplished with a wrecking ball, but the current value of scrap metal slowed the demolition to a delicate reclamation project. The towering backhoes and power shovels looked like dinosaurs picking through a human ruin.

Without the old Ford plant blocking the view, the breathtaking panorama of the airport spread out before me. A flickering line of jets assembled from the eastern horizon to the west. Swimming low in the airfield, they silently touched down one after another. Meanwhile, the baby shuffled and jabbed visibly under my shirt, riled up by the sugar. Something was being born here, and I wasn't sure what it was or what it meant to my new family making a home near the airport.

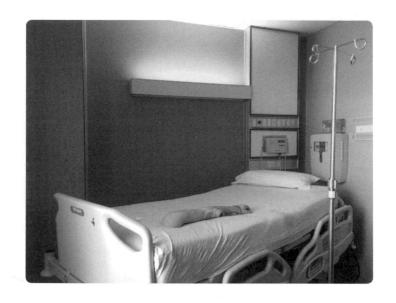

Former postpartum room at South Fulton Hospital, 2016.

TWENTY

BIRTHDAY

It came as no surprise to anyone but me that I didn't find my houses, but I did, amazingly, have a baby. Guy was born at our neighborhood hospital in April 2011.

I chose South Fulton Medical Center because it was close—only a mile from our house. It was a small, aging community hospital with a surprisingly low C-section rate and a new neonatal intensive care unit. Nothing fancy, but perfectly sufficient for the uncomplicated natural birth I planned.

When you're part of a certain demographic—college-educated, insured, savvy consumers the place where you "plan to deliver" is as carefully selected as daycare or a piece of real estate. Barring an emergency, you can shop around, tour hospitals all over the region, interview staff, and otherwise curate the birth experience. In the last trimester of pregnancy, I did just that. I found a midwife practicing water birth and hired a doula. I wrote a detailed birth plan, then designed it and printed copies on lime green cardstock so the nurses would read it. I chose a hospital in East Point because it seemed like the next best thing to a home birth. I didn't plan to stay there long.

Jason and I toured the maternity ward at South Fulton one evening after work. Obscured by expansions over the years, the hospital is a complex of modernist slabs rising on a hilltop that we drove by almost every day. As we got closer, I could see that a recent facade paint job masked the original blonde brick and decorative concrete screen blocks. I knew it was a small hospital, and the two-level parking deck, half-empty, confirmed this. We followed two other couples to a small visitors' area in the Women's Center and waited while a wall-mounted flatscreen played to a half circle of mauve and teak chairs.

The wide steel doors to the labor and delivery area buzzed and swung open. A nurse with startling false eyelashes introduced herself and told us she'd been at South Fulton for twenty-five years. We trailed her like ducklings through a progression of rooms, from triage, to labor and delivery, to the mother baby units to the NICU. She explained that they delivered only a few babies each day so we would have the undivided attention of the nurses and staff. "Rock-a-Bye Baby" would play over the public address system when our child was born. All of this sounded pleasant to me, but I saw the woman who was expecting twins exchange a concerned look with her husband.

Once upon a time, South Fulton was one of Atlanta's premier maternity centers. I learned that my uncle David was born at South Fulton Hospital in 1963, the year it opened. My grandmother's account of her fifth and final birth sounded like a nightmare. She was drugged and restrained, despite assurances from the doctor that she could be awake during delivery.

"You still felt the pain, but you just wouldn't remember it," she said, frowning.

My grandfather would have been pacing the waiting room, barred from labor and delivery by those steel doors. I compared this mental image to my parents' "Soromundi Course" in 1978. "Dads and Moms Stick Together" and all that.

Instead of reading online reviews, I dug up a brief history of South Fulton Hospital at the East Point Historical Society. Founded by a coalition of community leaders from East Point, College Park, and Hapeville to serve the burgeoning Tri-Cities, the hospital was built on the site of an African-American church called Graball and a nameless "colored" settlement. At the groundbreaking ceremony in 1961, white ladies in horn-rimmed specs and beehive hairdos posed cross-legged while the gents made speeches and brandished ceremonial spades by a field of kudzu.

The project struck me as another example of early 1960s slum clearance and urban renewal, part of the post-war boom announcing that Atlanta had big-city aspirations and economic muscle. The hospital was conceived and constructed at the same time as Atlanta's first shopping malls, interstate highways, and skyscrapers. In 1961, Mayor Hartsfield's Atlanta Municipal Airport opened just as Ivan Allen Jr. was campaigning for mayor and promising to build a stadium for major league sports downtown. Those landmarks of modern Atlanta were demolished long ago; somehow South Fulton is still standing.

Delivering babies was always a defining role for the hospital and a symbol of optimism for the community. A 1979 history of South Fulton waxed poetic on the significance of the facility: "The first baby born at the new hospital had the last name of Smith, a name indicative, some feel, of the universality of support for this new community project."

By 1988, according to its 25th anniversary marketing materials, South Fulton was "Atlanta's finest" maternity hospital, delivering 1,500 babies a year. (In 2013, Atlanta's Northside Hospital led the entire nation by delivering 27,000 babies.) A multi-million dollar expansion in the 1980s brought new "birthing rooms" to South Fulton for a more "homey-type atmosphere." In addition to offering the proud parents a free infant car seat, the hospital gave them the "opportunity to share a moment of privacy by providing them with a steak dinner for two in a special dining room."

I could picture the hospital's evolution from the sterile, doctor-centric environment where my Granny was compulsorily sedated to a slightly warmer approach. This shift was driven not so much by cultural expectations, but by the lucrative and competitive business of delivering babies. Today the perks at South Fulton included an inflatable birthing tub and a recently renovated waiting room. That's okay, I thought. No way could I eat a steak dinner after giving birth anyway.

The morning of my due date, Jason and I went to the midwife's office for a final checkup. I had switched to Marsha Ford's practice late in pregnancy in order to deliver at South Fulton and it generally seemed that I was her only white patient. The staff knew my name and Jason's name. Her patients, all African-American women, mostly from the neighborhood, waited in rocking chairs and chatted about their pregnancies while a small television in the corner played videos of water births. My eyes started leaking every single time they lifted a cheese-smeared, scrunchy infant from the pool. I got to know the videos and the other patients during our long waits to see Marsha between deliveries.

That morning I was referred to the hospital for a high-level ultrasound. Jason and I waited in the windowless basement of South Fulton for what felt like hours, watching CNN and wondering if we had been forgotten. There were parts of the hospital that clearly had not been updated since the 1960s. Here the framed watercolor prints and maple-toned faux wood abruptly ended and the original walls, institutional grey, began. I actually preferred the mid-century clocks, the honest materials—stainless steel, enamel tile, and real wood—but it was jarring to see the change.

Finally, I had the ultrasound, which looked okay to the tech, but you can never trust the techs, with their well-practiced poker faces. They always let the doctor give you the news.

During our brief drive home, my mobile phone lit up: the midwife's office.

"Come on up to the hospital," her receptionist said, friendly but without any small talk.

"We just left the hospital," I said.

"It's time to have the baby," she sang. "Now."

Despite forty full weeks of neurotically researched and documented pregnancy, I was unprepared for this announcement. The midwife saw the scans and made the call: She was concerned that the baby was measuring small. I was being induced. While Jason threw our bags in the car, I wandered into the kitchen and made a sloppy peanut butter sandwich. Then I left it, whole, on the counter.

Our homey-type birthing room was painted an earthy brown and apricot, with two wide windows overlooking the parking deck and a stand of pine trees. We stayed up late that night watching reruns on yet another hospital television set. Jason tried to stretch out in a thin vinyl recliner that may have been around since the hospital opened. I waited to feel something, for the induction meds to kick in.

The next morning, I woke up to the crampy beginnings of a long labor. By mid-morning, I was halfway dilated and had already run through the "pain management" techniques learned in childbirth class. Contractions, which I had previously only seen on television, fucking hurt. I suddenly had all this time to study the pain up close, burying my face in it. As labor progressed, I shed what remained of my clothes, my sense of decorum or humor or justice, my vocabulary and taste in music, my politics and faith, the time of day, the name of the president. The birth plan was a distant memory. I told Jason I wanted drugs.

The midwife called to check on me around lunchtime. She told me to go take a shower, to walk the hallways. I tried to match her calmness. Jason distracted me with his iPod playlists—Classical, Baroque, indie-folk—all annoying. He held my hand up and down the hallways, mumbling reassurances. This is normal, this is good, this is a baby coming out of your body.

Around noon, the doula showed up, trailing peppermint oil. She taped my birth plan by the door, dimmed the lights, and fed me honey through a straw. I don't remember much. Have I mentioned the pain? I remember shards, the fine clarity of the two minutes between contractions. The hands on the clock were a focal point. Hours passed.

Later that afternoon, Marsha arrived in full midwife regalia, all dreadlocks and a flowing blue dashiki. She was so glorious, so commanding, I wanted to go through with the birth plan just to impress her. She pulled the monitor off my belly, barked orders to the nurses, who obeyed. "She's Marsha's patient," they whispered, which made me feel fearless and favored. I got dispatches from the waiting room where our families were gathered, taking bets on the baby's name, time of birth, and birth weight. One contraction followed another. I got in and out of the tub.

It took several hours of maneuvering in every conceivable position to get the baby out. I've always been bookish, so athletic metaphors fail me here. All I can say is that I exerted every muscle in my body, as intensely as possible, for much longer than I thought possible. Nurses, students, curious onlookers came and went. I overheard Marsha saying, "It's called maternal exhaustion." The treetops outside our window were thrashing around in the false evening gloom.

Fourteen hours after labor started, it finally ended when Marsha decisively hauled a baby out of my body near 9:00 PM. Not sure if he was crying or not. It was over.

In the contraband videos of Guy's birth, I look so wrecked, I can barely open my eyes to look at the small and smeary child on my chest. The baby's eyes were wide open, blue and blinking. I remember that it was a complete shock to find another person in the room. My mind was blessedly blank, the only thought tumbling across the littered void was, "Where did he come from?"

The next day, I learned that dozens of tornadoes had cut a path of destruction across the south overnight. Watching the news in our cramped postpartum unit, we caught up on Will and Kate's royal wedding and tornado wreckage across Tennessee, Alabama, Georgia and Mississippi. Guy's birthday was the climax of one of the largest super-tornado outbreaks in U.S. history, which killed more than 300 people.

A few weeks later, on our first family road trip to visit my mother in Tennessee, Jason and Guy and I drove past the spot in north Georgia where a tornado had drilled across I-75. On either side of the road stood a lane of trees mowed down mid-trunk. We passed a towering bouquet of blown-out logo signs, twisted and snapped by the force of it. Clusters of empty foundations and rubble dotted north Alabama. It sounds dramatic, but the sight of this terribly reorganized landscape became an enduring part of my memories of childbirth.

South Fulton Medical Center closed its Women's Services department the next summer. In 2012, the hospital operator consolidated South Fulton with another facility and all labor and delivery patients were transferred to the other hospital. The paper reported that South Fulton was "financially ailing," and the operator attributed the closure to "continued reimbursement decreases that make it difficult for smaller hospitals with lower volumes to operate this service line."

Not enough patients chose South Fulton, or not enough with insurance cards, so South Fulton ceased providing one of its key services to the southside. It stopped being a place where people are born. Uncle David was one of the first babies born at South Fulton Hospital in 1963. My son, in 2011, would be among the last. Where did he come from? I saw that question in a new light.

What is a community hospital that doesn't deliver babies? An ER with a lot of empty space upstairs? South Fulton Hospital changed names a few times as it changed hands between operators. With each new regime came a proliferation of new logos and wall plaques, new administrators and promises. The only ones who remember the history of the place are the maintenance men. They let me into the deserted Labor and Delivery wing because I asked nicely to visit the room where I gave birth. They didn't ask a single question, just swiped a key card over the panel to open those steel doors.

I looked over the empty bulletin boards and brochure racks in the long and vacant hallways. It was all silence and stillness in the middle of a hospital. I could hear my own heart pounding as I peered into each of the small rooms, looking for the one with red-clay walls and dual windows full of treetops. I found Room 6 and snapped a few photos. It was completely bare and of course it felt smaller than I remembered.

Is it odd that I wanted to find the room? I only spent a day there, but the amount of time doesn't matter. "Surely *feelings*," as Eudora

Welty put it, "are bound up in place. The human mind is a mass of associations—associations more poetic even than actual." A breakup can happen on a street corner, a first kiss on a doorstep. The death of a dog, the birth of a baby; they happen in small, sterile, institutional corridors. We are not supposed to care, but those places become storied. Historic.

Watching planes in Hapeville, 2015.

TWENTY-ONE

OBSERVATION DECK:
Five Years Later

For her sixtieth birthday, Mom was considering a sports car. Father's Day coincided with her birthday, so instead of buying a car, she treated herself and Jason to the "Porsche Driving Experience" at the new Porsche North America headquarters by the airport. Part upscale brand immersion, part carnival amusement, for $450 per person, the "driving experience" included an hour and a half in a 911 Turbo on their 1.6-mile test track with a professional driving coach.

This test track was part of the new "Porsche Experience Center," built on the site of the old Ford assembly plant. The $100 million, twenty-seven-acre corporate headquarters was developed in close collaboration with the FAA to fit snugly within the buildable space and height restrictions of a site by the runways. The building loomed glassy and aerodynamic, a sleek and muscular arc that seemed to have landed on the northeast edge of the airport. Designed to make an impression from the air, the campus was a titanic billboard for the hundred million passengers taking off and landing from Hartsfield-Jackson every year.

The replacement of the Ford assembly plant, which made the middle-class dream attainable to a generation of Atlantans, with a luxury car company struck me as a kind of odd poetry. I noticed that the signs for Henry Ford Avenue were changed to Porsche Avenue in time for the ribbon cutting.

I waited with my sons, ages two and four, on a high observation deck while Daddy and Gramma whizzed around below on the track. The brightly colored cars looked like toys on the manicured obstacle course.

My sons. They are never still, but they were riveted by the grand noise and combined marvel of the racetrack and runways. I watched the back of their heads, swiveling to follow the cars. The older one was tall and skinny, with insubordinate blonde hair. His little brother, a head shorter, was round and dimpled, with blonde curls. They were boys now, not babies. Four years into motherhood, emerging from the ferocious blur of sleep deprivation, it still felt somewhat dangerous for me to be in charge of them. This suspicion was amplified as airplanes landed in front of us, close enough to thrash the treetops. The jets grew larger as they approached from the east, focusing from a warbly light in the distance to an enormous, juddering shell of steel, blacking out the sky.

The toddler, stocky but sensitive, leapt into my arms as the sound wave passed through our bodies. His brother, realizing that we had survived, shouted, " 'Bye, airplane!" and searched the horizon for the next arrival.

We rambled along the length of Porsche's observation deck where I could see that the back of the U-shaped office building was a clear span of windows, providing every office with a panoramic view of the airport. From this vantage point, the airfield spread out before us. The grass strips between the runways were bright as Astroturf. The sky never looked this big in Atlanta.

The test track was sandwiched between the runways on one side and Interstate 75 on the other. Just beyond the ten-lane stream of cars, I could see a stand of planted pines where Plunkytown used to be, a newish off-airport parking compound called FastPark on the threshold of Mountain View. The southern end of the test track featured a huge digital billboard which marked, I now knew, the entrance to an ill-conceived subdivision called Fairfax. For a brief period between 1949 and 1967, there were 200 houses clustered between the runways, like a tidal island that was eventually submerged.

Since then, airport planners have been more vigilant, insisting the only thing that belonged close to the runways were heavy industrial plants, landfills, warehouses, or parking lots. But here was this gleaming corporate headquarters nestled by the airport and actually facing the tarmac, as if it could improve its luxury brand by being associated with the precision, horsepower, and spectacle of its neighbor.

It is weird to think that my children are from here, this shifting non-place at the crossroads of the world. Still, growing up near the airport has its distinct thrills. These last few years, I have been prowling for a good place to watch airplanes land and take off at Hartsfield-Jackson, both for the boys and for myself. I wished for an observation deck, a perch unobstructed by fences and warning signs. The airport is an enormous operation, but it's hard to get a sense of the whole. At 4,700 acres, the airport delivers the kind of vast vista that Atlanta sorely lacks. We don't have waterfront views, or any kind of vantage point for the city. What we do have is a massive airport.

Though the official "driving experience" was a pricey affair, it was not lost on me that Porsche's four-star restaurant, also overlooking the runways, was open to the public. The best airport views were always found in exclusive private spaces—hotel rooms, corporate boardrooms, and the Delta Elite SkyClub. By designing spaces that are open to the public, the Porsche Experience Center suggested that the airport edge can be a dazzling public space.

Eventually the boys grew accustomed to the noise, slightly hypnotized by the relentless pace of all those well-choreographed take-offs and landings, one every few seconds. I trailed them through the Porsche Café and the Porsche Museum, wiping fingerprints off the glass and chrome displays with my shirt. When Jason and my mom rejoined us in the lobby, she was ebullient; he was white with motion sickness.

My mother, divorced from the chef, had finally discovered the pleasures of long-term commitment in the form of a successful catering company. She had built a commercial kitchen on the back of her property in Tennessee and spent the next two decades enhancing her home and gardens and business.

But it is in her role as grandmother that she truly mastered the art of staying put. After choosing the surprisingly traditional moniker "Gramma," she stopped coloring her hair, letting the gray swirl into her natural light brown. Before I had kids, I had doubts that I would have maternal instincts and no expectation that she would suddenly become grandmotherly. I was surprised at our new routine. Gramma came to visit in Atlanta every other week, bringing flowers and groceries for me, wind chimes and trinkets for the grandbabies. She was prepared to babysit and fold laundry and hold little boys on her lap for as long as they would sit still.

AIRPORTS ALL OVER THE WORLD from Frankfurt, Germany to Japan had generous public observation decks. Why did these airports do it? Why invest in an amenity that does not directly move passengers, or benefit airlines?

In the jet age, when aircraft were even noisier and nastier than they are now, people lined up to watch the action at airports. Any time I talked to pilots, they had an origin story about spending time at an observation deck as a child, watching the airplanes for hours. The curious public was not so weary of air travel; airports were not so hostile towards the general public out of security concerns.

Observation decks satisfied an early public relations agenda for the aviation industry, and along the way, became really interesting communal spaces that inspired a generation of pilots, flight attendants, and air traffic controllers. But they also served as a friendly link between the community and the airports themselves.

I had tried to watch planes from the upper floors of the Airport Hilton, restaurants on Virginia Avenue, spots along Main Street in

College Park, and from the elevated MARTA train. It was not unusual to see people pulled over on the side of Loop Road to watch and take photos. These people get the cops called on them. They look like terrorists. All these ad hoc observation decks felt risky, like trespassing. And none of them provided a very good view.

This airport doesn't integrate with its surrounding communities; it has some very impressive walls and fences. For decades, the surrounding cities have been hunkered down, trying to protect themselves from airport noise and expansion. The Porsche Experience made me wonder what it would look like if they turned their faces (and storefronts and parks) back towards the runways.

Before Google Maps, it was virtually impossible to see the airport unless you were looking down from the window of an airplane. With social media, it became possible to follow the Instagram feeds of pilots and air traffic controllers, allowing neighbors like me to see a whole different world "inside the fence." This is the closest thing we have to an observation deck or a public interface at the airport.

As Atlanta grows, matures, urbanizes, gentrifies, there will be a whole generation thinking critically about our public spaces and our infrastructure. In cities across the nation, there is a growing demand for better design in urban environments. And people like me, the children of the displaced, are asking more critical questions about the airport's cost, such as, what is the cultural impact of all this expansion?

Since the Olympics, the Atlanta airport has been strictly focused on efficiency and maintaining that title of "the world's busiest airport." Year after year, Hartsfield-Jackson Atlanta International Airport barely hangs onto this title. The center of global aviation is shifting with the global economy, and new airports in Beijing and Dubai are poised to surpass Atlanta in the next decade. Istanbul is targeting the "world's busiest" title and building a new airport that can handle 150 million passengers a year, with room to expand.

What does it mean to our soul that our city is the busiest in the world? Atlanta has been "too busy to hate," but also too busy to care, to invest, to get attached to our civic landmarks and icons. What happens when we outgrow being the world's busiest? We'll have this massive hunk of infrastructure and we'll have to find a new title for ourselves. Could we be the "world's easiest" airport? Most beautiful? Most approachable? Most integrated?

Currently, the airport earns that ranking as a hub for connecting flights. Counting the passengers who actually arrive and depart in Atlanta, the numbers are more like a small regional airport, like Zurich. What if the airport was a destination, not just a place you pass through as quickly as possible?

In the last decade, the airport has expanded to burst out its former boundaries, the interstate highways. To the south, the Fifth Runway extends dramatically over interstate I-285. To the west, an automated people mover called the SkyTrain carries passengers over I-85 to a new rental car center. And on the east, the new Maynard H. Jackson International Terminal creates a new entrance to the airport from I-75.

This is fascinating to me because the airport isn't a contained fortress anymore. It is permeable. It is no longer this hub located on the outskirts of a city with homogenous development like logistics, warehouses, conference centers, some offices, all the stuff that supports aviation. As it breaks out of the confines of the interstates, the airport is increasingly linked to the urban fabric of the city at large.

What if it were more fully integrated with the community, both physically and psychologically? I imagine bike lanes that stretch from downtown Atlanta to the terminal. Imagine public spaces that bridge the moat around the airport, portals or observation decks. A true public space that's not just for "post-security" passengers waiting for a flight, or Porsche-driving elites, but open to all and free of admission. Something as sweeping and grand as the airport itself.

The link between a world class airport and the surrounding community should go beyond the physical connections. Small businesses and schools close to the airport should benefit from its economic vitality. There should be virtually no unemployment next to the state's largest employer. The best schools in Atlanta should be near the city's chief economic engine.

"Airport urbanism" is just good urbanism. It's about accepting that the airport is part of the city, not a machine on the outskirts. The area around an airport should work like a city works, that is, adapt and grow organically, containing the multitude of mixed-use ingredients that people need, from cafes to car washes, schools and clinics, and a range of places to live. I started out wishing the airport had an observation deck, but more than that, I wish it had an observation-deck mentality—more open, civic. More opportunities for joy.

LATER THAT SUMMER, a friend texted me some photos from Mountain View. They showed a freshly cleared demolition site: a yellow backhoe parked beside a bulldozer, a plain of combed red dirt, and a tidy stack of broken concrete slab.

I knew right away it was the lot at the corner of South West Street and Old Dixie Highway. I could tell by the angle of a jet aiming up and over the blank backside of a low warehouse. I've spent a lot of time with that one ivy-eaten oak tree, its top branches honeyed by the sunset. It was the site of the last remaining house on the last remaining corner of the street where I used to live.

For me, that house was the prototype. A tool to imagine what the block used to look like when houses occupied both sides of the street, and the streets all around it. The old bungalow, stout yet modest, stood in for my missing house.

The back of my neck felt hot as I flipped through the photos. It felt like a particularly large bill had finally arrived in the mail. You stand there in the street for a little too long, vaguely wishing you could mend the torn envelope, close the mailbox, return to sender. It was a dirty shock, but it could hardly be called a surprise.

They tore down Dell Air.

I have been observing the steady erasure of this block for years. I've been to this spot many times, always in search of some clue about what happened to my house. Now the boys sit strapped in their car seats as I pull over on the side of the road to explore the latest demolition site. I roll down the windows and ask them to sing a song for me so I can hear them as I drift through the rubble.

What began with residential buyouts continues today with the clearing of commercial properties. It's a slow process, imperceptible to the average passerby. Just one of a hundred projects on the endless Georgia Department of Transportation project list. The demolition seems to happen in slow motion, or in the night. I never actually witness the backhoes in action. I just cruise through and another Mountain View artifact is missing, fresh asphalt in its place.

A month later, Blanchard's Bakery caught fire, despite its location two blocks from Clayton County Fire Station #9. It did not reopen.

Aside from that clawed-up, unsettled feeling, it's no surprise, because the plans are out there; they're public record. Mountain View has been at the top of Clayton County's list of redevelopment projects for over a decade. While it may look like a good place to dump tires, in the eyes of a planner, Mountain View has a list of advantages. Clayton County's Economic Development Director called it "the last great green, developable area inside the perimeter."

It's a shaky pitch. Mountain View is not a blank slate. The only "green" swaths fall between the rows of warehouses, when summer kudzu unfolds across the ruins of the old neighborhoods.

Still, the location, wedged between freeways and flight paths, is ideal for logistics firms, freight-forwarders, and government agencies like the FAA. This proximity to the airport once made it an undesirable place to live. Now that's the chief selling point. Clayton County is betting its economic future on these haunted acres.

I found a Georgia Department of Transportation map that shows how Mountain View will be transformed from derelict "noise land" into a transportation hub, connecting the new international terminal ("Atlanta's Front Door to the World") on the west with I-285 to the east. At the center of these plans is the new Southern Crescent Multimodal Transportation Center, a proposed commuter rail line that would connect Atlanta to Macon and take traffic off the highways.

Even when you know the plans are out there, it's jarring when it happens. A decade is a long time to wait, for rumors to drift, for people to protest, then dream, to be converted, then forget what the planners pitched. Planners can study and propose ideas, but they have no authority to build. It could take years for market conditions to align.

In ten years, a baby becomes a fifth grader. In ten more, that kid is gone, his childhood home fixed in memory. Meanwhile, the eraser is a lumbering thing.

According to the map, Mountain View's main streets, Old Dixie and Conley Road, will be relocated. A constellation of red dots marks structures for demolition, including Dell Air. Many of the buildings pictured in the base map are already gone. There will be nothing left of the original Mountain View community, except the occasional reunions, organized on Facebook, that take place at the restaurant in the Farmers Market.

The red dots are precise and final; a glaring period that puts an end to all my words.

ACKNOWLEDGEMENTS

Thanks to all who have supported my preoccupation with this subject and contributed to making this book possible. First, I am grateful for the unconditional love and encouragement of my parents Jesse Slagle, Gayle Slagle, and Jayne Slagle, my longsuffering allies Myra Slagle Oviatt and Lowell Slagle, and all the Palmers. Home is wherever y'all are.

This book started as a thesis project at the Sewanee School of Letters under the spell of John Jeremiah Sullivan and wise guidance of John Grammer. I appreciate the backing of David Leedle and Wayne Whitesides during those summers in Tennessee. Special thanks to everyone who shared their stories and friendship: Harold Benefield, Eddie Buckholts, L.C. Cole, Gary Cooper, Mike Earles, Dawn Edmonson, Dell Thompson, Beverly Martin, Rusty and Debbie Stovall, and Tara Taylor. My chief enablers include Dr. Brennan Collins, Ryan Gravel, Johnathon Kelso, and Jeff Williams.

The team at Hub City Press have been warm and courageous creative partners. I am beyond grateful for the vision of Betsy Teter and Meg Reid in both book publishing and city-making.

Endless gratitude to Jason Palmer, my first and best reader, a fine specimen of Forest Park manhood who is beloved everywhere he goes.

**HUB CITY PRESS**

HUB CITY PRESS is a non-profit independent press in Spartanburg, SC, that publishes well-crafted, high-quality works by new and established authors, with an emphasis on the Southern experience. We are committed to high-caliber novels, short stories, poetry, plays, memoir, and works emphasizing regional culture and history. We are particularly interested in books with a strong sense of place.

Hub City Press is an imprint of the non-profit Hub City Writers Project, founded in 1995 to foster a sense of community through the literary arts. Our metaphor of organization purposely looks backward to the nineteenth century when Spartanburg was known as the "hub city," a place where railroads converged and departed.

RECENT HUB CITY PRESS TITLES

Over the Plain Houses • Julia Franks

Suburban Gospel • Mark Beaver

Minnow • James E. McTeer II

Pasture Art • Marlin Barton

Punch. • Ray McManus

The Whiskey Baron • Jon Sealy

The Only Sounds We Make • Lee Zacharias

In the Garden of Stone • Susan Tekulve